# Japan's hidden Christians

# Japan's hidden Christians

by Ann M. harrington

A Campion Book

Loyola University Press
Chicago

Loyola University Press
3441 North Ashland Avenue
Chicago, IL 60657

Cover and interior design by Nancy Gruenke

**Library of Congress Cataloging-in-Publication Data**
Harrington, Ann.
  Japan's hidden Christians/by Ann Harrington.
    p. cm.
  Includes bibliographical references and index.
  ISBN 0-8294-0741-3
  1. Christians—Japan.   2. Missions, French—Japan.
3. Japan—Religion.   I. Title.
BR1305.H35   1992
275.2'07—dc20                                        92-27035
                                                     CIP

*To my families*

# Table of Contents

# List of Maps and Tables

# Acknowledgments

This work began a number of years back as my Ph.D. dissertation. Over the years, I have continued my interest in Japan's hidden Kirishitan, with the hope that someday I'd be able to tell the story for a wider audience. Thanks to Loyola University Press, this hope has become a reality. The National Endowment for the Humanities awarded me a summer seminar in Japanese history with Professors Albert Craig and Harold Bolitho at Harvard University in 1990, which afforded me some extra time to work on the manuscript. I am grateful to Harold Bolitho for encouraging me to publish this work. For help in the early stages of the work, I owe thanks to Professor Peter Duus. Professor Joseph Kitagawa and Fr. Joseph J. Spae, C.I.C.M., offered helpful suggestions and provided me with key contact persons, as did Dorita Clifford, B.V.M. Fr. Diego Pacheco, S.J., introduced me to the late Professor Kataoka Yakichi. Professors Tagita Kōya, Ebisawa Arimichi, and the late Furuno Kiyoto also met with me while I was in Japan. Fr. Jean Vérinaud, M.E.P., Archivist in Paris for the Société des Missions-Etrangères de Paris, received me most graciously. My friend, Kurohashi Yasuko, has given me much support in this project and I am deeply grateful to her.

Special thanks to Professor Joseph A. Gagliano, the chair of the history department at Loyola University, for providing me with time to work on this book; to the editors at Loyola University Press for their suggestions and improvements; to Dolores Perez for typing the manuscript on disk; to the Loyola University Center for Instructional Design for preparing the maps; and to my colleagues now at Loyola University from the former Mundelein College who have always shown interest in my work, especially Joan Frances Crowley, B.V.M., Prudence Moylan, and Paula Pfeffer. I am indebted to my B.V.M. Congregation, first for assigning me to study

Japan; and thereafter, for giving me the freedom to pursue my studies.

Finally, my deep gratitude to my parents who would have loved to see this in print; to my sisters and brothers, for their interest; to my extended family, Marianne Littau, Jean O'Keefe, Kateri O'Shea, and Mary Christina Stretch for their patience and presence over the years; and especially to my local B.V.M. family, Kathleen Conway, Mary Pat Haley, and Mary Alma Sullivan who have contributed to this project in many untold ways.

Whatever errors remain in the text are mine alone.

# Introduction

For more than two hundred years, while Japan was relatively isolated from the Western world and Christianity was strictly forbidden by the Tokugawa Bakufu (which was in power from 1603 to 1868), a small group of Japanese Catholics endeavored to keep their faith alive underground. Despite persecution and bloodshed, they succeeded in transmitting Christian teachings through seven generations. When Catholic missionaries were again permitted to enter Japan in the nineteenth century, they discovered small pockets of Christianity in Kyūshū, the southernmost of Japan's four main islands, and immediately looked toward wooing these descendants of Japan's first Christians back to an orthodox practice of Roman Catholicism. Some members of this underground movement accepted the teachings of the newly arrived Catholic missionaries. Others, however, numbering about 30,000, refused, and they continued to live their own brand of Christianity, practicing what they believed to be the true faith as communicated to their ancestors in Japan's first Christian century, 1549–1639. This study will look at those Christians who refused the advances of the French missionaries.

The choice of terminology in the study presents a problem. The first Catholic missionaries to return to Japan were members of the Société des Missions-Etrangères de Paris (M.E.P.), and it was members of this group who first referred to the Christians of concern here as *les séparés*, in Japanese, *hanare* (separated). Japanese scholars studying the subject vary in their choice of terminology. Tagita Kōya,* in his detailed study, uses the term *sempuku* (hidden), following the example of his mentor, Anesaki Masaharu.[1] Kataoka Yakichi[2] and Furuno

---

* Japanese names in the text will be cited in the Japanese manner, surname first, with the exception of endnote entries.

Kiyoto[3] both prefer the term *kakure* (hidden). The term *sempuku* in Japanese implies more a hiding out of fear or necessity, whereas *kakure* can mean hiding or concealment by choice, the desire to remain anonymous.

For this study, the term *kakure* will be used because it does not convey the pejorative sense implied by the term *hanare* and because it aptly describes the way these Christians preferred to carry on their religious practice, i.e., in secret. It is customary to use the word *Kirishitan* (Christians, the Japanese pronunciation of the Portuguese *Christão*) when talking about the kakure Kirishitan, to distinguish them from present-day Japanese Christians.

Any attempt to understand the kakure Kirishitan raises a number of questions. What were the Christian converts taught from 1549 to 1639? How did they camouflage their Christian practices after 1639, when discovery meant certain death? How did their beliefs and practices change through seven generations? How did the nineteenth-century missionaries react to them? This study proposes to look at each of these questions in an attempt to prove the validity of three hypotheses. (1) The Christianity that went underground and was continued after the Tokugawa period by the kakure Kirishitan was more closely aligned with the practice of Christianity during Japan's first Christian period than was the practice demanded by the French missionaries after 1865. (2) The religion of the kakure Kirishitan bears out certain theories of cultural change, namely: (a) "the form of a new culture element is more readily accepted than its associated meaning because form is more easily observed and imitated than meaning"; and (b) "new traits are accepted primarily on the basis of their utility and their compatibility with the existing cultural configuration."[4] (3) The religion practiced by the kakure Kirishitan in the nineteenth century incorporated many elements characteristic of traditional Japanese religious practice, such as the harmony of humankind, gods, and nature; the importance of ancestors; the significance of charms and ritual; the prominent place of festivals and local cults; and the close relationship between religion and everyday life.[5]

This work serves as an introduction of the kakure Kirishitan to the English-speaking world. Much research remains to be done on this topic. The study relies heavily on research done by Japanese scholars, primarily the works of Tagita, Furuno, and Kataoka, and on the writings of the French missionaries. It will begin, however, with the advent of Christianity in Japan.[6]

Chapter
I

# The Advent of
# Christianity

# bistorical Background

The Catholic missionaries who arrived in Japan in 1549 came armed not only with the spirit of adventure but also with a sense of holy zeal sparked by the religious controversies raging in Europe. In 1517, the Augustinian monk Martin Luther had posted his Ninety-Five Theses of reform on a church door in Germany, and, by the middle of the sixteenth century, England, the Scandinavian countries, part of Switzerland, and most of Germany and the Netherlands had severed their ties with the Roman Catholic church.

As a result the Catholic church began a long-overdue self-scrutiny, a reform of its own. Begun as an attack against the "altered" doctrines and the questioning of papal authority that eventually emerged from the posting of the theses, the reform also attempted to rid the church of the many abuses that had initially motivated Luther's attack, such as nepotism in the church hierarchy and the sale of indulgences.

The convocation of the Council of Trent (1545–1563) marked the most influential step taken in church reform. Its aim was "to assure the integrity of the Christian religion, the reform of morals, the concord of Christian princes and peoples, and the means of repelling the attacks of infidels."[1] And it was at the height of this religious turmoil in Europe and the attempts of the Catholic church to renew its inner spirit and place of predominance that the missionaries set out to preach Catholicism to "heathen" peoples. They were trying to fulfill the gospel command to "go forth and teach all nations," and also to add more members to the ranks of the church to make up for the many who had fallen by the wayside in Europe.

Japan, at this same time, was going through an era of great unrest. The title of *shōgun* (military leader) was held by the Ashikaga family, but by 1549 the country was actually divided up into a number of domains ruled by local lords, or *daimyō*.* Begun as military defense units, these domains gradually became administrative centers. When the last Ashikaga shōgun was deposed in 1573, his passing went almost unnoticed; the Ashikaga power had evaporated.

The daimyō, who by the sixteenth century had become absolute rulers in their own domains, governed with an iron hand. They demanded loyal service from all their subjects, from the military services of the warrior class (samurai) to the heavy taxes and labor exacted from the peasant farmers. The first Europeans to arrive in Japan in the sixteenth century referred to the daimyō as "kings."

As is always the case in periods of great change, religious sects, which could transcend the troubled times, gained in popularity. The Zen Buddhist sects demanding strict discipline and promising sudden enlightenment were popular among the samurai. The Nichiren and Shin sects, assuring salvation through the Lotus Sutra and Amida Buddha, made many converts among the common people.

But perhaps much more common were those Japanese whose religious beliefs would fall within the category of folk religion. With minimal knowledge of the intricacies

---

*Ordinarily Japanese nouns are not inflected for singular and plural; context usually clarifies whether a noun is singular or plural. For example, *daimyō* can refer to one or several daimyō.

of Buddhism and Shintō, the majority of the Japanese at this time satisfied their spiritual needs by blending aspects of these religions into their everyday life and into the festivals and ceremonies and taboos they had been taught by their ancestors.

The times, therefore, were favorable to the introduction of yet another spiritual means of coping with life's hardships, and given the political situation of the time, no group was better suited to introduce Christianity into sixteenth-century Japan than the Society of Jesus, the Jesuits. The founder of the Society of Jesus, Ignatius Loyola, had been a military officer and used some military terminology in the rule for the order and in his *Spiritual Exercises*, a foundational Jesuit document, which one author has called "a religious manual of arms."[2] The purpose of this company was the conquest of souls under the banner of Christ the King. The papal bull, *Regimini Militantis Ecclesiae* ("To the Governance of the Church Militant"), which legitimized the Society as a religious order on September 27, 1540, echoes the military imagery.

Ignatius conceived the idea of placing his small band at the service of the pope, and the members of the new order expressed a willingness to go anywhere in the world to gain souls for the Kingdom of Christ. It was a timely move, considering the crisis caused by the Protestant Reformation, for the new Society thus had the backing of the most powerful figure in Roman Catholicism and consequently the backing of the European kings who had remained faithful to the Roman church.

The Jesuits, says church historian Philip Hughes, were the "most perfectly subordinated instrument the papacy has ever had at its disposal."[3] And they became, in time, a very powerful and influential religious order.

Francis Xavier, one of the original seven members of Ignatius' small "army" (and a fellow Basque), set sail for Japan with two other Jesuits, Cosme de Torres and Juan Fernández, and arrived in Kagoshima on August 15, 1549.

Accompanying the Jesuits was a samurai named Yajirō, who had fled from his native Satsuma on a Portuguese ship in 1544 after killing a man and had taken refuge in Malacca. It was in Malacca that he met the Jesuits, learned Portuguese, and was converted to Catholicism. He agreed to return to Japan with the missionaries and to act as their interpreter.

# Approaches to Missionary Activity

The missionaries appraised the political situation rather quickly and realized they would have to deal with the various daimyō in Japan in order to reach the people. Their first proselytizing in Japan, then, began with the elite of Japanese society and worked its way down to the common people. The missionaries also had to come to terms with the fact that the majority of the daimyō who welcomed them did so because with the religion came the possibility of trade with the Portuguese merchants.

Along with the political and economic situation, the missionaries confronted a culture radically different from their own. They faced problems in the choice of language used to convey the Christian message; in how to proselytize—to strive for numbers of converts or for in-depth instruction on a limited scale; in determining how much to teach the Japanese of Catholic beliefs and practices; and in deciding how to adapt their life-style and ritual to the Japanese culture. We will discuss how the missionaries came to terms with each of these problems.

## Language

The first hurdle the missionaries had to overcome was quite obviously the language problem. Not only did these Europeans not speak Japanese, but the Japanese language did not contain words that could translate adequately some of the concepts central to Christianity. With the young Yajirō acting as interpreter, Xavier and his co-workers had some painful and rude awakenings.

During their first days of preaching, Yajirō used the word *dainichi* to translate "God." What Xavier did not know was that dainichi was one of a number of representations of the Buddha and not a Japanese term for an all-powerful, creator-God. The Japanese, in fact, had no such religious concept.

Other Buddhist terms used by the missionaries proved equally confusing. *Hotoke* was another term used for "God," and again it referred to the Buddha. *Tamashii* was used for "soul," and this word in Japanese made no distinction between vegetative, sensile, or rational soul. The missionaries themselves were called *sō* (*bonzes,* monks), and the Christian teaching was called *Buppō,* "the Law of Hotoke."[4]

Understandably, Japanese began confusing the Christian teachings with Buddhism, and many thought this "new" religion was just another sect of Buddhism. Hubert Cieslik, a Jesuit specializing in Japan's early Christian period, observes that "the official document whereby Ouchi Yashinaga bestowed the property of the old Daidoji in Yamaguchi on the missionaries in 1552 tells us that 'The bonzes (sō) who have come from the West in order to preach the Law of Buddha (*Buppō-shōryu no tame*) are hereby authorized to build that temple.'"[5]

These misunderstandings brought the missionaries to the realization that their interpreter, Yajirō, had only superficial notions of Buddhism and furthermore that he was uneducated. His Japanese was the patois of his native area of Satsuma, and his ability to read and write Japanese was at best minimal.

To clear up these misunderstandings resulting from their choice of language, the missionaries saw two alternatives, either to continue using Buddhist terminology and giving a Christian interpretation or to retain foreign terms for concepts that had no Japanese equivalent. They chose the latter and brought Latin and Portuguese words into Japan's religious vocabulary. For example, God was rendered as *Deus* (in Japanese script, *Deusu*) and soul was rendered as *anima*. The Catholic priests came to be called *bateren* (from the Portuguese *padre*). This practice was common by 1555.[6]

## preaching

When confronting the question of whether to strive for breadth or depth in their preaching, the missionaries realized that the interest the local daimyō evidenced in Christianity was coupled with an interest in engaging in trade with the Portuguese. With the trade came Christianity, or conversely, with Christianity came the Portuguese trading ships. Japanese history scholar George Sansom remarks, "It has often been said that 'The Jesuits wished to use trade for the Kingdom of Heaven and the Japanese wished to use the Kingdom of Heaven for trade.'"[7] It was difficult therefore for the missionaries to assess the sincerity of the Japanese who showed an interest in Christianity during these early years. What was clear was that many Japanese turned out to listen to the preaching, and more converts were made during the first century of Christianity in Japan than exist today.

The large numbers of early converts posed two major problems for the missionaries, especially when a daimyō commanded that all his followers receive baptism: (1) how could the small number of missionaries meet the needs of the growing numbers of converts? (2) How knowledgeable were the new converts about Catholic doctrine, especially those who had converted for the profits of trade or at the command of their daimyō? These questions were a cause of concern to the missionaries and eventually to their headquarters in Rome.[8]

The discussion centered on the question of whether the missionaries should concentrate their efforts on making a small number of converts who would be thoroughly indoctrinated in the faith or whether they should strive to convert a large number and worry later about deepening the level of instruction. This latter approach was referred to as the extension method of conversion.

Those who felt that the extension method of conversion was dangerous argued their case on three points. First, some Japanese converted because they wished to please their daimyō and yet had little preparation for baptism. Second, after baptism, many continued their pagan ways. Finally, it was argued, this method did not follow the example of the Apostles, who never baptized before thorough catechization. Those who defended the extension method refuted the first argument as not being objective or accurate. In reference to the second, it was agreed that one cannot expect too much from a new convert. On the third point, those who defended the extension method disagreed outright, saying that the extension method was indeed the way the Apostles had gone about making converts.[9]

Further insight is gained into the attitudes of the missionaries when we consider four other reasons given for making as many converts as possible. Those favoring the extension method argued that it is better to have Japanese in the church even if they are not well prepared; that they will provide a supportive atmosphere for their fellow Japanese Christians; that the extension method will lead to the conversion of more daimyō, who with their laws would help the cause of Christianity; and that the more converts that are made, the more money there will be to build churches and schools.[10]

Underlying the eventual acceptance of the extension method of conversion were certain beliefs and expectations. One important church doctrine that the missionaries and their superiors in Rome were conscious of was the teaching that without baptism there is no salvation. This teaching had been re-emphasized at the Council of Trent in 1547. It was clear to the missionaries, therefore, that in order to save the Japanese they must convert as many of them as possible. It is also important to remember that the missionaries expected to expand their forces in Japan and that they therefore emphasized oral preaching. This was considered more important than the sacraments (with the exception of baptism). The deepening in faith and understanding, they felt, could be left for post-baptismal instructions.

Another reason that made breadth more important than depth was the constant threat of war in the domains where the missionaries were working, and, toward the end of the sixteenth century and into the seventeenth century, there was also the threat of persecution. It was therefore necessary, they argued, to convert as many as possible in a given area before the missionaries were forced to move on. They took precautions, however, in case they might have to leave an area suddenly. They instructed Japanese lay teachers called *dōjuku*, and established sodalities or confraternities of believers (in Portuguese, *companhia*).

The dōjuku (fellow lodgers) served two purposes initially. They were to help the missionaries in responding to the needs of the numbers of Japanese requesting instruction, and, as natives of an area, they were to remain even if the missionaries had to flee. They were asked primarily to preach and catechize. By 1592, there were more than five hundred dōjuku.[11] Below we will discuss their role as baptizers.

The sodalities were composed of groups of Christians who would meet together to pray, to reaffirm their beliefs, and to offer support to one another. These groups helped the Christians to keep their faith alive, and eventually, helped them face the horrors of martyrdom.

Given the above arguments and the precautions taken, the missionaries felt justified in employing the extension method of conversion. With the optimism and faith characteristic of Christian missionaries, they believed that God would take care of "God's own." And they saw baptism as just one step in an ever-deepening Christian life.

# Teachings

Through their missionary experiences in India and in their early contacts with the Japanese, Xavier and his followers had devised a basic three-stage catechetical process that outlined the order of the teachings: pre-evangelization, catechumenism, and formation.

During the pre-evangelization period the listeners were to decide whether or not they were interested in Christianity. Three teachings were stressed in this period. The first was that there can be no salvation in any Japanese sect; included in this first stage was a "logical refutation of the potential convert's particular sect."[12] The second was that there is only one God, Creator, who has given the human race the law of salvation. The third was that the soul is immortal and, in the life after death, those who recognize God and live according to God's law will be eternally blessed while those who do not recognize God will be condemned.[13]

The second stage centered on catechizing, or explaining in more detail the teachings of the Catholic church. Included here were the teachings on the mystery of the Trinity; the creation story, the fall of the angels, and the fall of Adam and Eve; the salvation of humankind through the death and resurrection of Jesus Christ; the last judgment, at which time individuals would either be accepted into heaven or condemned to hell; the Ten Commandments; the sacrament of penance; the necessity for absolute loyalty to the church; and the reception of baptism after the potential convert was told its significance.[14]

The catechizing process was aided, after the movable-type printing press was brought to Japan by the Jesuit Alexandro Valignano in 1590, by printed manuals for the instruction of Christians. The first such work printed in

Japanese characters was the *Doctrina Christan*, dated 1592. The book consisted of twelve chapters written in the form of questions and answers, discussing the things it was important for a Christian to know, such as the meaning of Christian doctrine; prayers, among them the Sign of the Cross, the Our Father, the Hail Mary, the Salve Regina, and the Apostles' Creed; the Ten Commandments; the precepts of the church; the seven capital sins; the sacraments; and other teachings such as the corporal and spiritual works of mercy, the theological and cardinal virtues, and the gifts of the Holy Spirit.[15]

The missionaries kept the teachings as simple as possible and avoided introducing any of the controversies or theological disputes current in the church.[16] They also tailored the teaching to the persons they were addressing. The common people were given the simplest and briefest instruction. The length of instruction might vary from two to forty days, but the average was one week to ten days.[17]

The ideal toward which the missionaries strove was to allow baptism only after the potential converts had detested their "pagan" rites, persevered in the laws of God, and shown contrition for their sins.[18] Because of the numerous instances of mass conversion, it was impossible for the missionaries to judge whether they had reached their goal with each convert.[19]

The brief encounter the missionaries had with many of their converts forced them to give slight attention to some aspects of the Christian doctrine. With the exception of baptism, the sacraments fell into this category. A thorough instruction on the meaning and significance of the sacraments was subordinated to an understanding and practice of the Ten Commandments. The sacraments were not stressed as a way of deepening the believer's communication with God; they were seen rather as simple aids.[20]

The notion of church as institution was also downplayed. It is not evident that the catechumens saw themselves as members of the church. This was a concept that was reserved for a later period of deeper indoctrination. Along the same line, church law was not emphasized, because the missionaries did not want the new converts to identify Christianity with a set of laws, and they urged caution and discretion in making the people obey Canon Law.[21] Alexandro Valignano, the Jesuit superior of the Japanese mission, declared that it was not his intention that the failures of the Japanese Christians to observe the precepts of fasting, keeping holy Sundays and feastdays, and hearing Mass on those days be treated as mortal sins.[22]

The third and final stage of the catechetical method was that of formation. In this stage of their proselytizing, the missionaries looked toward a careful cultivation of the faith of the new converts and further instruction on the sacraments and on the laws and precepts of the church. During this period of formation, the converts would also be led to deeper understanding of the doctrines of the church. As we will see, this last stage of the catechetical process never materialized.

## Adaptation

Another aspect of the early missionary period that must be considered in this study is adaptation on the part of the missionaries. They had entered a culture that differed markedly from their own European culture, and substantial difficulties arose for Japanese and European alike. The resolution of the cultural clash directly affected the success or failure of their preaching in various areas of Japan; this clash ranged from the life-style of the missionaries to their administration of the sacraments.

Since the missionaries had determined it essential to win the favor of the influential segment of Japanese society, the problem of dress arose almost immediately. Xavier learned of its importance by experience in 1550, when he went to Kyoto to seek an audience with the emperor. He had the notion that if he could obtain the permission to preach from the highest authority in the land, all the daimyō would have to bow to the emperor's wish. Arriving poorly dressed and bearing no gifts, he was refused entrance. His next visit, which was to a daimyō in Yamaguchi, found him dressed in an impressive costume, and he presented the daimyō exotic gifts of a clock, spectacles, a musket, brocade, and mirrors. In return, the daimyō publicly proclaimed Xavier's right to preach in his domain.[23] In the early years of the mission, this example of adaptation was the exception, not the rule.

Francisco Cabral, mission superior from 1570 to 1581, believed that "the Japanese would have to adapt themselves to the Portuguese Jesuits and not vice versa."[24] He reversed the early adaptive tendencies of Xavier and had the Jesuits return to wearing their black robes as opposed to adapting to the local custom of silk robes worn by Japanese of commensurate position. Asian specialist George Elison sees this as "yet more exotica" on the Japanese scene and adds that Cabral succeeded in offending commoners, samurai, and daimyō alike.[25]

Cabral's biggest blindspot was his unwillingness to allow Japanese to enter the Society of Jesus as equals and to train for ordination to the priesthood. In 1596, well after the Jesuits had begun training Japanese for the Jesuit priesthood and Cabral had been out of Japan for some seventeen years, he wrote:

> If one does not cease and desist admitting Japanese into the Society . . . that will be the reason for the collapse of the Society, Nay! of Christianity, in Japan, and it will later hardly prove possible to find a remedy. . . . I have seen no other nation as conceited, covetous, inconstant, and insincere as the Japanese.[26]

With the arrival of Alexandro Valignano in 1579, in the position of official visitor, a reversal trend started, and

Cabral eventually resigned his post and left Japan in 1580. Valignano made a quick assessment of the Japanese mission and immediately set out to begin reforms. He insisted on the organization of systematic language study for the missionaries where Cabral felt that it was impossible to learn Japanese sufficiently well to preach to pagans.[27] He then directed the Jesuits to adapt themselves to the Japanese life-style in dress, cleanliness, diet, rank, and dwellings. Finally, he directed that seminaries should be built to train Japanese for the priesthood.[28]

A more important adaptation came in the administration of the sacrament of baptism. Because of the church teaching that there was no salvation without baptism, the missionaries taught lay people how to administer the sacrament. The original intent had been to use lay baptizers and Jesuit brothers in this ministry, even outside of cases of necessity. Although there was some ambiguity, necessity ordinarily meant when there was danger of death. In such cases, the priest was to be notified, and if the trip would take him more than two or three days, the baptizer was allowed to administer the sacrament. In cases of extreme necessity, anyone could baptize.[29]

Lay people given special tasks were the *dōjuku*, discussed above, and the *kambō*, a Buddhist term for monks who care for the temple. The kambō were less attached to the Society than were the dōjuku, and their task was to care for the churches. They read to people and taught them the prayers. The kambō were assembled once a month, and taught the formula for baptism and for contrition at death.[30]

The administration of baptism was not always carried out according to the exact formula, which normally required that the convert (or child) be anointed with holy oil. For several reasons, this portion of the ritual was often omitted. First, it was difficult to obtain sufficient blessed oils, since there was seldom a bishop in Japan and bishops were the only ones empowered to bless the oils. Second, there were complaints among the Japanese

Christians when they realized that some Christians had been anointed and others had not; this caused envy among converts and doubts about the validity of the sacrament when anointing was omitted. Finally, there was a certain modesty among the Japanese, especially the women, in exposing their chest and back for anointing.[31]

Rules for the administration of baptism were set by Luis Cerqueira, a Jesuit who arrived in Japan in 1598, the second and last bishop to set foot on Japanese soil during this early Christian period.[32] Although he wanted to fulfill all the ceremonies that the church prescribed, he was open to omitting what was strange to the Japanese and anything that would offend their extreme sensitivity. He therefore made several changes in the baptismal ceremony for adults. First, he allowed the priest to make the sign of the cross over the kimono of women in respect for their sense of modesty. He said it was unnecessary to touch the saliva of the person to be baptized, as was the custom; to touch the lips and make the sign of the cross from a distance was sufficient. The salt to be placed on the tongue of the new Christian could be gathered in a little spoon and placed in the hands of the initiate, who would then put it in his or her own mouth. For anointing with oil, a small instrument was to be used in order to avoid direct contact. The laying of the baptizer's hand on the head of the initiate was acceptable because it did not offend the Japanese sense of decency. With children, the administration of the sacrament followed the liturgical form used in the West.[33]

These adaptive tendencies on the part of the Jesuits can be explained partly by their need to ingratiate themselves with the political powers and partly by their proselytizing experiences in India, where they had also encountered a highly cultured people.

# Life of the Early Christians

An evaluation of the religious life of Japan's early Christian converts, their level of religious instruction, their religious practices, and their access to the sacraments of the Catholic church, placed in the context of the times, is revealing. Japan was still in the throes of civil war when the missionaries arrived in 1549, and the war raged until the time of Tokugawa Ieyasu's rise to military hegemony as shōgun in 1603.

Consequently, Christian preaching and practice in the early years had to rely on the fickle whim of the individual daimyō. The entire first half of the Christian century emerges as one lacking stability, when Christianity never achieved an easy, certain, working relationship with the political powers. There was the ever-present knowledge that missionaries might have to escape to a new area and that Christians would have to face the decision to apostatize, flee, or die.

Religious life was therefore organized with this thought in mind. In the absence of priests, religious duties were entrusted to the dōjuku, who helped out around the churches and the priests' residences and were also called on to preach, catechize, and instruct Christians. They did not take religious vows but they shaved their heads, wore a kind of cassock, and devoted themselves to the service of the church. Elison observes

that they were not given any formal training.[34] Within
the various Christian villages the kambō, besides caring
for the churches when the priests were absent, were
"entrusted with the task of instructing the children in
Christian doctrine and reading spiritual books for the
congregation on Sundays and feastdays. They visited the
sick, called the priest for the dying, baptized children in
danger of death, and presided at the funeral services."[35]

In 1603, the number of kambō had reached 170.[36]
When one considers the ratio of ordained priests to
Japanese Christians throughout the early years, it
becomes quite clear that great responsibility was vested in
these lay helpers. For example, in 1579 the ratio of priests
to Christians was approximately 1:5,652; in 1588, 1:5,
128; and in 1614, 1:3,061.[37] One must also bear in mind
that the Christians were scattered in various parts of the
country and therefore regular visits to each Christian
community were impossible.

Administration of the sacraments is restricted in
Catholic teaching. Practically, a priest was needed for
penance and the eucharist, for anointing the sick and for
witnessing marriages; a bishop was required for ordina-
tions and normally for confirmation. Only baptism could
be administered by someone not ordained. It is apparent,
therefore, that the sacramental life of these early converts
was irregular. In some areas, like Hirado, Ikitsuki, and the
Gotō islands, the Christians were sometimes left several
years without access to the priests. Attendance at Mass
and the reception of the holy eucharist was therefore
impossible. At these times, the Christians would assemble
in the church or in the home of a Christian and listen to
a sermon by a dōjuku or readings by a kambō or another
layman. Heavy stress was put on the recitation of prayers,
celebration of feastdays, penitential practices (such as fla-
gellation) during Lent, and solemn funeral ceremonies.[38]

The sodalities (or compania) were also important centers for maintaining Christian beliefs and practices in the

absence of priests. There were sodalities of the Blessed Virgin (*Santa Maria no gumi*) started by the Jesuits, Confraternities of the Cord (*Obi no gumi*) begun by the Franciscans, and Confraternities of the Rosary (*Rozario no gumi*) under the direction of the Dominicans.[39] These groups later coincided with the *goningumi* system, consisting of mutual surveillance units developed by the Tokugawa government, which will be discussed below.[40] After 1614, when persecution began in earnest and all the churches were destroyed or confiscated, religious gatherings had to be held in secret in the homes of Christians.

Religious articles also played an important part in the faith of the early converts. The missionaries distributed these articles to remind the Christians of their beliefs, and to encourage steadfastness in their religious duties. Some Japanese Christians would walk miles to obtain rosary beads.[41] The rosary became so popular, in fact, that one missionary is quoted as saying, "I don't know if there is another nation in the world that esteems and venerates as much the holy beads."[42] At the time of baptism, in some areas, the newly initiated Christians would bring in their Buddhist beads, which were burned, and would in return be given a Christian rosary.[43]

Other objects that were popular were wax images of the victorious lamb (a symbol of Christ) with an image of a saint on the reverse side. These were popular among the Portuguese sailors of the time as a remedy against storms. Converts relished articles and objects that they could hang in their homes, such as printed representations of Christ and Mary. They also exhibited a strong devotion to the cross. Some Christians wore relics around their necks.[44]

The new converts also showed great devotion to the baptismal water. They believed it was the water that effected cures. Even non-Christians would send for the holy water when ill, believing it had medicinal and spiritual value.[45] The father general of the Jesuits insisted on the missionary and apostolic function of miracles, and Valignano did not deny the existence of miracles in Japan in cases of diabolic possession or illness.[46]

With these external signs, the converts did begin to get a superficial knowledge of Christianity. However, the time counted on by the missionaries for deeper instruction never materialized. Thus the converts' concept of being members of an institutional church never took hold. A full sacramental life, which the church considered essential for growth and development of a healthy Christian life, was impossible.* Apart from baptism, sacramental celebrations could not take place without ordained ministers. Holy orders, in fact, required a bishop, as did confirmation generally in those days. The only time a bishop was in residence in Japan during this early period was from 1598 to 1614, so very few Japanese Christians ever received confirmation,[47] and the development of a native Japanese clergy hardly got off the ground. In 1614, there were only seven native diocesan priests and a mere handful of Japanese Jesuits.

A similar problem existed with the sacrament of penance, which also required a priest. According to church teaching, if one had committed a mortal sin and died without confessing it, one could be damned to hell for all eternity. The priests therefore had circulated a pamphlet called *Konchirisan no ryaku* ("A Compendium of Contrition") to assist the Christians in the absence of a priest. Divided into four parts, the work explains the necessity of confession, instructs the Christians to read the work when they have sinned and have no access to the sacrament of penance, and explains how Christians could save their souls if they express true sorrow even though no priest was available to give absolution. It also contains instructions on which parts to read to a person who is sick and to a person who is dying. In cases of

---

* The Catholic church recognizes seven sacraments: baptism, penance, holy eucharist, matrimony, holy orders, confirmation, and the anointment of the sick, which earlier was called extreme unction (last rites).

extreme necessity, when there is little time, the Christians are instructed to read only the prayer at the end of the pamphlet.[48] The *Konchirisan no ryaku* also had to substitute for the sacrament of extreme unction (last rites).

The surviving printed copy of the *Konchirisan no ryaku* is dated Keichō 8 (1603), and although only the title page is in existence, a number of handwritten copies discovered in the nineteenth century are believed to be faithful to the original.[49]

As far as the sacrament of matrimony is concerned, there does not seem to be any indication that the Christians were given special instructions on how to make marriages that would be recognized by the church. This presented a problem to the French missionaries in the nineteenth century. It will be discussed in chapter 5.

The care taken by the missionaries to prepare the Christian converts to continue the faith in their absence is impressive. But even the most pessimistic of the priests and Japanese Christians could not have imagined the fury that would be turned loose on Christianity nor the length of time that Christians would be forced to survive on their own.

# Persecution

The missionaries carried the constant hope that as the years passed they would increase the number of converts in Japan, but they also looked forward to a continuing influx of missionaries and to the ordination of a growing number of Japanese into the priesthood. They looked forward to completing what they had merely begun, namely, a thorough indoctrination of their new converts, exposing them to a deeper understanding of Christianity.

This optimism of the missionaries received a blow, however, as the Japanese authorities became increasingly suspicious of the motives of the missionaries and the "double loyalty" of the Japanese Christians. Troubles began in the last quarter of the sixteenth century. Through the military genius of three relatively obscure men, Oda Nobunaga (1545–1582), Toyotomi Hideyoshi (1536–1598), and Tokugawa Ieyasu (1542–1616), Japan moved toward national unification. Under Hideyoshi, military reunification was completed by 1590, but it was left to Ieyasu to establish the political regime, legitimized by the emperor in 1603, which would hold Japan together in relative peace until 1868. From the time of Hideyoshi on, however, the fate of Christianity was in the hands of a single authority; the days of courting the favor of an individual daimyō were over.

The first ban on Christianity was issued by Hideyoshi on July 24, 1587.[50] He gave the missionaries twenty days to gather their belongings together and leave Japan, but he allowed for the continuation of Portuguese trade. Because Hideyoshi did not enforce this edict, missionary activity continued; but from this time on, the missionary work was impeded by sporadic persecutions throughout Japan. There was a period of relative freedom from harassment after Tokugawa Ieyasu's success in 1600 at Sekigahara, the scene of a crucial battle in which Tokugawa Ieyasu was victorious over Hideyoshi's heirs, thus establishing the ascendancy of the Tokugawa family and making it possible for Ieyasu to become shōgun in 1603. Missionary exploits continued. This proved, however, to be the lull before the storm.

On January 27, 1614, another edict banning Christianity was issued by the successor and son of Ieyasu, Tokugawa Hidetada.[51] This edict demanded the immediate deportation of all foreign missionaries, and the local daimyō were instructed to destroy Christian churches and to force Japanese Christians to return to their national religions. The beginnings of Japan's hidden (kakure) Christians can be dated from this edict.

Rewards were offered for leading the authorities to Christians, the amount of the reward varying (between 1614 and 1716) from five hundred to two hundred pieces of silver for a *bateren* (priest); three hundred to one hundred pieces of silver for an *iruman* (brother); and one hundred to fifty pieces of silver for a dōjuku.[52]

Some missionaries went into hiding among the Japanese Christians or disguised themselves as Portuguese merchants. But the final blow came in a series of edicts issued between 1633 and 1639, which ultimately closed off Japan from the outside world, with the exception of the Dutch and the Chinese.[53] The major impetus for these drastic measures was to rid Japan of Christianity and all it implied—religiously, politically, and morally.

The suppression of Christianity was carried out with a thoroughness and consistency that underlines the evil that the Japanese leaders felt the foreign religion would perpetrate. A Christian Suppression Office was established in 1640 (*Kirishitan Shūmon aratame-yaku*) by order of the shōgun, and Christians were actively and systematically sought out for execution. The first method of detection was the above-mentioned rewards system. The second operated through the goningumi system. A *kumi* consisted of five or more households and served as a vehicle for keeping order on the local level. In relationship to Christianity, it was a mutual surveillance unit, and each member of the kumi was responsible for reporting any Christians in the group. Discovery of an unreported Christian meant that each member of the kumi was liable to the same punishment meted out to the Christian.[54]

The ceremony of *e-bumi* (picture treading) was yet another means of detection. All Japanese were obliged from time to time to trample on a sacred Christian image, such as an image of Christ, of a cross, or of the Blessed Virgin Mary. Paper images eventually were replaced by large copper medals, which were more durable.[55]

Finally, each family was required to register at a Buddhist temple, become a member of a Buddhist sect, and obtain a temple certificate. Originally, this law applied only to areas where there was a heavy concentration of Christians, but in 1659 the law covered all Japanese.[56]

In the midst of these persecutions Christians were instructed on the excellence of martyrdom in copies of Christian manuscripts that circulated first during the persecutions of 1597–98. The work "explains the meaning of martyrdom, its dignity, its utility and its conditions . . . what intention and with what preparation it must above all be faced under the present threatening conditions."[57]

It is generally accepted that in 1614 there were approximately 300,000 Christians in Japan. By the time of the final *sakoku* (closed country) edict in 1639, it is estimated that there remained about 150,000 Christians. The early periodic execution of Christians together with the later systematic arrests and executions claimed approximately 2,126 lives between 1549 and 1650, the greatest number being killed between 1614 and 1639.[58] There were also large numbers who apostatized. Japan scholar C. R. Boxer concludes that a "much higher proportion of *heimin* (peasants, artisans, and merchants) than of samurai remained faithful unto death."[59]

Hence, the majority of those who sustained the faith, the common people, were those who had received the most elementary instruction, and this leads one to conclude that those Japanese Christians who went underground did so with an extremely limited understanding of their newfound faith. With the average length of instruction less than two weeks, only the most basic elements of Christianity could have been conveyed.

Many of the Christians who went into hiding, losing all contact with the missionaries and the institutional church, succeeded in transmitting their Christian heritage through seven generations. The next three chapters will examine the life and practices of the descendants of Japan's first Christians.

**Map 1
Japan**

# Map 2
# Ikitsuki Island Area

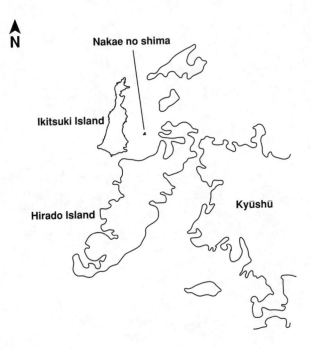

# Map 3
# Ikitsuki Island

N

Gosaki

Moridakesake

Ichibuura

Sakaime

Sato

Nake no shima

Yamada

Tachiura

Chapter
II

# The Kakure
# Kirishitan

# Introduction

There are no records or documents detailing the life of the Christians who began to go underground in 1614 and totally submerged themselves in 1639. What happened over the course of two centuries can only be surmised from what emerged in the nineteenth century. Although it was not until the 1930s that any in-depth study of the surviving Kirishitan was undertaken, one can assume, based on the observations made by the French missionaries in the 1800s (see chapter 5), that the kakure Kirishitan first studied by Tagita Kōya in the 1930s were practicing their religion much as they had practiced it when Japan once again opened its doors to the West. In this chapter we will introduce the various kakure Kirishitan settlements and their officials, and then look at two practices that were common to all kakure Kirishitan groups: baptism and funeral services.

In the second half of the nineteenth century, there were about 30,000 to 35,000 kakure Kirishitan, living for the most part in poor farming and fishing villages. They resided exclusively in the southern part of Japan, in Kyūshū and its offshore islands. The largest concentration of kakure Kirishitan was found in Ikitsuki, a small island off the northwest coast of Kyūshū. There were also kakure Kirishitan villages in Hirado, a larger island southwest of Ikitsuki; in the Gotō Islands, located in the Japan Sea, directly west of Nagasaki; and in Kyūshū proper, in the Kurosaki area (now encompassed in the region of Sotome-mura), about fifteen miles northwest of Nagasaki.

The kakure Kirishitan in each area practiced their beliefs in isolation from the surrounding areas, and had little or no contact with other kakure Kirishitan settlements. Tagita, in his detailed study, sees two broad groupings of kakure Kirishitan on the basis of their beliefs. In the Gotō Islands and in the Kurosaki area, the *higurichō* or *ochō* (calendar) was central to the belief structure. In Hirado and Ikitsuki, the *nandogami* (closet gods) were central to belief and practice.[1]

The higurichō of the Gotō Islands and Kurosaki was believed to have been transposed from the solar calendar of 1634, which was the last printed calendar sent to Japan and circulated there by the missionaries.[2] According to the legend popular among the Kirishitan of Kurosaki, the man responsible for learning how to make the calendar was Basutean (Sebastian). He was born in the early seventeenth century in Nonomaki, outside of Nagasaki. Raised in a Buddhist temple, where he served as a porter, he converted to Catholicism under the direction of a Spanish priest named Juan and became his catechist.[3]

When the priest died, Basutean did not know how to determine the Christian feasts, so he fasted for twenty-one days (in some accounts, seventy days). Juan appeared to him and told him to take the feast of the Annunciation (March 25) as the beginnings of his deliberations, the feast marking the halfway point of the season of Lent. This feast would fall toward the spring equinox on the lunar calendar, and since the season of Lent lasts forty-six days, he could determine the movable Christian feasts, such as Easter, which occurs when Lent ends. The *chōkata* (calendar maker) of the kakure Kirishitan was believed to be passing on this calendar devised by Basutean.[4]

Basutean was executed in 1657. The kakure Kirishitan of the Gotōs and Kurosaki observed the twentieth and twenty-third of each month as Sundays, in honor of the day that Basutean was condemned to death and the day he was executed.[5]

The place of prominence afforded Basutean and, similarly, the chōkata is easily understandable in terms of Japanese tradition. During the reign of Prince Shōtoku (573–621) the Japanese had adopted the Chinese calendar, so important in Confucian tradition. Only with a correct reading of the heavens, it was believed, could a ruler be certain he was governing his earthly realm correctly and in harmony with the heavens. The importance of the calendar was reiterated as late as 1751, when the shōgun Yoshimune issued a calendar that had been determined by a commission of Japanese scholars (as opposed to copying the Chinese calculations) and proclaimed the new era of Precious Calendar (*Hōreki*).[6] The importance of the calendar and the calendar maker for the kakure Kirishitan reflected the long Confucian tradition, which has been so influential in the cultural and political life of East Asia, while the content of the calendar, as we will see, reflected the teachings of the missionaries.

*Nandogami in a household altar*

For the kakure Kirishitan of Ikitsuki and Hirado, the nandogami replaced the calendar as the focus of religious worship. The term *nandogami* (closet gods) referred to special objects treasured by the kakure Kirishitan on Ikitsuki and Hirado. Tagita outlines six categories of nandogami that he found on Ikitsuki.

The first group, called *gozensama*, consisted of hanging scrolls or banners depicting Christ, Mary, martyrs generally recognized by the Church, special martyrs from Ikitsuki, and saints. Also in this category were metal statues of the Blessed Virgin Mary and woodblock prints of Christ on the Cross.[7]

*Hanging scroll*

Next were the small wooden plaques representing the fifteen mysteries of the rosary. These were kept in the home of one of the officials, and their use will be discussed below.[8]

The third group consisted of the holy water (also called *San Juan-sama*, the *sama* a suffix of highest respect), the container used to collect the water, and the stick used to sprinkle it on persons, on food, or in homes to bless or cleanse. The stick was called *izuppo* (from the Portuguese *isoppo*, hyssop), from the biblical passage, "There was a jar there, full of common wine. They stuck a sponge soaked in this wine on some hyssop and raised it to his lips." (John 19:29)[9]

The fourth type of nandogami was called *otempensia* (from the Portuguese *penitença*, penance). Originally it referred to a bundle of hemp ropes, used by the Christians to inflict pain on themselves as a means of self-discipline. The Christians began to make these otempen-sia during the season of Lent, adding one piece of hemp rope each day, so that at the conclusion of Lent the bundle had forty-six ropes.[10] This item was also called *odōgu* (tool) and by the nineteenth century was used to expel demons from the sick and from the home.[11]

The fifth category of nandogami was *omaburi*. The omaburi were small pieces of paper cut in the shape of a cross, used as charms to protect homes, fields, and people. Tagita believes that these may have had some connection with the eucharist (sometimes called *Osuchia*), noting that they were treasured in small, unusual boxes not dissimilar to the containers used by Catholic priests to carry the eucharist to the sick or to persons at a distance.[12]

Finally, there were the *tamoto kami* (sleeve gods). The tamoto kami were objects of worship that the kakure Kirishitan tucked unobserved in the sleeve of a kimono, and these *kami* (gods) were sometimes small crosses cut out of paper, or a rosary.[13]

All of these nandogami were reminiscent of the religious objects so popular among the early Christians. The religious articles distributed by the missionaries were blessed, and they were to be treated with reverence. For many of the Christians, so often left without the services of the priests, these items constituted the most concrete reminder of their faith. Because there could be no eucharist or eucharistic service without the priests, it is understandable how these nandogami became gods for the kakure Kirishitan and came to be worshipped and treated with a reverence that Catholics reserve for the eucharist. But within Japanese tradition, Anesaki Masaharu has observed that objects used in Japanese religious ceremonies were believed to have divine and magical efficacy.[14]

Besides the distinction on the basis of higurichō and nandogami, Tagita also distinguishes the different areas of kakure Kirishitan by the name that was most commonly applied to them, either by themselves or by outsiders. The Kirishitan of central Gotō were called *motochō* (original book or calendar); those of lower Gotō, *furuchō* (old book or calendar); and those of the Kurosaki area, *kakure*. The Kirishitan of Hirado and Ikitsuki were called *furu-Kirishitan* (old Christians).[15]

The similarities that were found among the kakure Kirishitan of the Kurosaki area and the Gotōs can be explained by the fact that in 1797, the daimyō of Omura, who governed Kurosaki, now in the Sotome region, sent a number of people to the Gotō Islands where that daimyō had requested settlers. Since there was persecution in the Kurosaki region, the move greatly benefited those who were Christians. By the nineteenth century there was no communication between the Kirishitan of the Gotōs and those residing in Kurosaki.[16]

# Officials

When the Christians were forced to practice their beliefs in secret and were eventually left without an ordained priest, they developed their own system of religious leadership. The importance of the different officials, all of them male, varied in relation to the center of worship in each group.

Generally speaking, in Kurosaki and the Gotō Islands, where the *higuricho* (calendar) was central to the belief of the Kirishitan, the most important official was the chōkata. After the seclusion policy went into effect and Christian works could no longer circulate, it was a major task each year to determine the religious feastdays. This became the job of the chōkata, and he devised the religious calendar each year, informing his followers weekly of the important feasts and special days approaching.[17] He usually had about ten families under his jurisdiction and was in charge of conducting funeral services and memorial services. In some areas this post was hereditary; the heir to the post, however, occasionally acted for his older relative before actually assuming the office.[18]

The *mizukata* (water official) had the duty of baptizing newborns. The idea was to have one mizukata for each group. The mizukata was ordinarily chosen from among the people and had a term of office lasting from three to five years. However, in the case of both the chōkata and the mizukata, these facts varied from village to village depending on local circumstances. The term *kambōyaku* was sometimes used and could refer to either the chōkata or the mizukata.[19]

These officials generally served without pay, but in the case of unusual expenses, such as communal meals on feastdays, the believers were asked to make offerings to defray the costs.[20]

In Hirado and Ikitsuki, where the nandogami were the focus of worship, the official titles and duties were somewhat different. Of all the Kirishitan areas, Ikitsuki maintained the most thorough organization, and it is on this island that greatest emphasis will be placed in this book. Therefore, before looking at the officials in Ikitsuki, let us look briefly at the beginnings of Christianity on this island.

The Jesuit Gaspard Viela began work on Ikitsuki in 1557 at the invitation of Koteda Sayemon, chief vassal of the daimyō Matsuura Takanobu, who controlled Hirado and Ikitsuki. In 1550, Xavier had received permission from Matsuura to preach in Hirado. Koteda and his family converted to Christianity in 1557, and in that same year an estimated eight hundred to fifteen hundred islanders did the same—an example of mass conversion at the request of the chief vassal.[21]

Koteda, taking the Christian name Antonio, proved to be an ardent Christian. He went about preaching Christianity to his followers and with Viela began a massive campaign to destroy the Buddhist temples on the island.[22] In 1599, Matsuura began a widespread persecution of Christians, and Koteda's son, Jerome, gave up his position of power on Ikitsuki and with his family and some six hundred followers fled to Nagasaki. The Christians who remained on the island suffered persecution from about 1609 onwards.[23] By the time Japan closed itself off to the outside world in 1639, virtually the entire island was Christian.

There were seven Kirishitan areas in Ikitsuki: Yamada, Sato, Sakaime, Moridakesaki, Gosaki, Tachiura, and Ichibu-ura. For the most part, the residents of the first five areas made their living by farming and the residents of the other two by fishing.[24]

The highest official among the Ikitsuki Kirishitan was the *sazukeyaku* (the one who administered baptism). When he had to travel to other villages, he carried a staff as the symbol of his office. The kakure Kirishitan called him *ojisama* or *ojiisama*, the standard titles of respect for a man and an older man respectively, both to indicate respect and to hide his official role. In some areas this post was hereditary, and a man served for a period of ten years. However, if the sazukeyaku's spouse died during his term of office, he had to give up the post.[25]

In the event that a sazukeyaku had to be chosen, the people of the area assembled to choose his successor. The person selected had to know the words of the prayer for administering baptism, and he had to be deemed a holy and religious man. When a man was selected, he was given the instruments for the administration of baptism. He then took rice and sake to the home of his predecessor and returned to his own home in such a way as to meet no *erenjamon* (heretics, from the Portuguese *heresia*), meaning he was not to meet anyone who was not of his faith.[26]

The office of sazukeyaku was not a full-time occupation, and the man holding the post was ordinarily either a fisherman or a farmer. Because his official duties took time away from his work, the people of the area showed their appreciation by offering him such things as wheat and rice and sometimes donations of money.[27]

Under the jurisdiction of the sazukeyaku were the *tsumoto*, or the homes that contained the nandogami. The head of the tsumoto was called *gobanyaku*. He was called *ottosama* or *oyajisan* by his followers, again, terms of respect. When there was more than one tsumoto under a sazukeyaku, the residences were called from highest to lowest *uwayado*, *nakayado*, and *shitayado*, their rank depending on the year that their home became a tsumoto, the first rank going to the house first selected as the tsumoto. The head of each tsumoto accordingly was called from highest to lowest, *gobanyaku*, *nibanyaku*, *sanbanyaku*.[28]

The origin of the word *tsumoto* is not clear, but it referred to a place of lodging; it was also called *oyaji*. Since it was the home that contained the nandogami, it was the most important meeting place, and it corresponded to a church. The homes chosen as tsumoto rotated from village to village every few years in the area of Yamada, but in Sakaime and Ichibu the post was permanent. The head of the tsumoto, because he presided over festivals, had to memorize a number of prayers.[29]

Finally, each tsumoto was composed of a number of compania (from the Portuguese *companhia*, also called *kumi* or *kogumi*), each of these headed by a *mideshi* (disciple). The number of compania under a tsumoto varied in the different areas; for example, there might be three tsumoto, comprising six or seven compania. The number of households in a compania likewise varied from two to twelve. The rank of each mideshi, as with the tsumoto officials, was determined by the year of his appointment.[30] All of the households forming one tsumoto were also referred to as *kakeuchi* (or *kakiuchi*). The compania were responsible for providing the living expenses of the sazukeyaku and funds for the festivals held in the tsumoto.[31] (See table 1.)

The compania were almost certainly related to the various religious organizations started by the missionaries in the sixteenth and seventeenth centuries, but this type of group meeting was also prevalent in Japan from medieval times in the *kō* system (fraternity or religious association). Hori Ichiro, a specialist in Buddhism and folklore studies, points out that kō was originally a term for a Buddhist lecture meeting but gradually came "to

## Religious Organization among the Kakure Kirishitan in Jkitsuki

| Religious groupings* | Officials* | Function |
| --- | --- | --- |
| | Sazukeyaku | Highest official—over all religious groupings |
| Tsumoto | | |
|   Uwayado | Gobanyaku | House the nandogami |
|   Nakayado | Nibanyaku | House the nandogami |
|   Shitayado | Sanbanyaku | House the nandogami |
| Compania | Mideshi | House the ofuda and host monthly prayer meetings |

*Listed in order of importance

## Table 1

indicate those present at a Buddhist lecture meeting and the members of a religious fraternity."[32] These confraternities also coincided with the goningumi system enforced under the Tokugawa Bakufu.

In most areas of Ikitsuki, the members of the compania met at the home of the mideshi on the first Sunday of every month. Each mideshi had at his home a bag containing sixteen *ofuda*, which were small pieces of wood, about 1" x 1½" in size, with a cross, a number from one to five, and some simple characters on the front. On the reverse side, there were characters that indicated either joyful (*oyorokobi*), sorrowful (*okanashimi*), or glorious (*gororiya-sama*). These pieces of wood represented the fifteen mysteries in the life of Christ and his mother, Mary, that were meditated on by Catholics during the recitation of the rosary. The mystery was written in whole or in part on the respective wooden piece, but very few of the kakure Kirishitan understood what was written there. The sixteenth piece ordinarily had the joyful symbol on it and the word *amen* written in *kana* (the Japanese syllabary). At the monthly meeting, the assembled members of the compania drew out a wooden piece and saw this as their fortune for the month; drawing one of the joyful ofuda was considered the most desirable. The practice of drawing out ofuda, called *oshikae*,[33] bears a strong resemblance to the practice of drawing a fortune at a Shintō shrine.

*Ofuda*

The wooden pieces undoubtedly came into existence as a mode for concealing the fact that the group was assembled to recite the rosary, so popular among the early Christians. However, beads were also a popular item in Buddhism.

The term of office of the mideshi varied. In some areas he served five or six years, in others, the post rotated yearly. The mideshi was expected to be able to recite simple prayers, but if he was unable to do so, anyone in the compania who knew how could do so.[34]

The men who performed religious services for the kakure Kirishitan can be traced directly to the early Christian period when the dōjuku, kambō, and catechists assisted the priests. They were authorized to instruct, to baptize, to conduct religious prayer meetings, and to assist the sick and dying in sorrow for their sin. In general, they were encouraged to do as much as was allowed the unordained minister when the priests were not available. The kakure Kirishitan officials performed these same tasks, seemingly without ever having tried to carry on those elements of Christianity that were forbidden to them without the assistance of a priest or bishop, i.e., eucharistic services, confirmation, and confession.

Tagita notes that in Ikitsuki the official hierarchy was similar to Catholicism, where the sazukeyaku corresponded to a bishop (he carried a staff) and the gobanyaku to a priest.[35] Furuno Kiyoto, on the other hand, sees a correspondence with the Buddhist hierarchy. The sazukeyaku he likens to the *chōrōkaku* (superior or elder), the tsumoto to the *dannadera* (head temple), and the mideshi to the *danto sōdai* (the representatives of the temple supporters).[36]

The ranking of the various officials based on their year of appointment, while it existed somewhat in the hierarchy of the Catholic church, was not church custom. But in Japan, "in contrast to other societies, the provisions for recognition of merit are weak, and institutionalization of the social order has been effected largely by means of seniority."[37]

In chapter 3 we will discuss various festivals observed by the kakure Kirishitan that will further explain the role of the officials, but first let us look at two practices common to all kakure Kirishitan in the nineteenth century: baptism and funeral services.

# Baptism

One of the most important practices among all of the kakure Kirishitan was the administration of baptism. In Ikitsuki, the request for baptism was usually made two weeks in advance, and the sazukeyaku then had to observe various taboos. For example, he was not allowed to touch the night-soil bucket or cattle. For one week before the baptism, he was not allowed to work, and for several days before the event he could not have sexual relations.[38]

The notion of infant baptism was retained in many of the kakure Kirishitan groups. At baptism, the child (or the adult) was given a baptismal name called *arima no namae* (from the Latin *anima* or the Portuguese *alma*, meaning soul, and the Japanese *namae* meaning name), and a godparent was required. In Ikitsuki, by custom, the godparent, or *heco-oya*, was of the opposite sex of the person baptized.[39]

The water for baptism was obtained from a small island off the coast of Ikitsuki called Nakae no shima, the scene of a number of martyrdoms in 1622 and 1624. The water from Nakae was called *San Juan-sama* for two men named Juan or Johannes who died on the island and whose deaths were believed to have conveyed miraculous powers to this water.[40] Thus, in the absence of holy water blessed by priests, San Juan-sama became the holy water for the kakure Kirishitan.

Baptism was the only sacrament administered with any regularity during the first Christian period, and its importance in kakure Kirishitan groups is evident. Seeing the waters of baptism as miraculous also dates back to the early Christian period, when it was believed that the blessed waters not only had the power to remove sin but also to heal the sick, a belief not discouraged by the missionaries.

The stress placed on baptism and the powers of the baptismal waters found easy company with the Shintō stress on ritual cleanliness. Cleansing ceremonies began in early Japan and were required after childbirth, menstruation, and contact with death or illness. In Buddhism also, and perhaps more directly, we can see how Japanese Christians would have found it easy to relate to baptism. Japanese religion scholar Carmen Blacker says, "The final and culminating stage of Buddhahood is suitably expressed by the baptismal *seikanjō*, water poured on the head, which figures so prominently in the initiation of the orthodox sects of esoteric Buddhism."[41]

# ƒuneral Services

A second important practice observed among all of the kakure Kirishitan was the funeral ceremony and the observance of the death anniversary. During the period of persecution, as mentioned above, all Japanese had to register at a Buddhist temple. The kakure Kirishitan of Ikitsuki, for the most part, maintained that membership, so their funeral service was a combination of their own personal religious beliefs and the official Buddhist ceremony.

When a person died, the *ojisama* (the sazukeyaku) and *ottosama* (head of the tsumoto) were notified immediately, and a monk from the head temple was also notified and invited to perform a Buddhist service. Prior to the arrival of the monk, the kakure Kirishitan chanted a series of prayers and holy songs lasting forty to fifty minutes, then placed a small paper cross under the kimono of the deceased, next to the skin. The remainder of the ceremony was left up to the temple.[42]

The death was commemorated on the third day after death, and then on the seventh, thirty-fifth, and forty-ninth days; special prayers were offered for the deceased during the entire forty-nine day period. Death anniversaries were also observed on the first, third, seventh, thirteenth, twenty-fifth, thirty-third, and forty-ninth years. These observances usually combined Buddhist and Christian elements.[43]

The missionaries had stressed the importance of a proper burial ceremony accompanied by prayers for the eternal salvation of the deceased. But once again, this was a practice that derived its importance from Japanese folk religion and Japanese Buddhism. As Hori points out:

> Japanese Buddhism has naturally tended to commingle with the folk religious elements, reinterpreting and systematizing them in various ways. The best example of this tendency is the fact that the most significant social function of present-day Japanese Buddhism, regardless of sect, is the funeral ceremony and memorial services for the spirit of the dead.[44]

Even for Japanese who have little or no need for Buddhism in their everyday life, the Buddhist funeral and memorial services are important at the time of death.

Hence, the practices of the kakure Kirishitan in dealing with death and burial, while showing a continuity with their Christian heritage, also show they were able to combine their new religious beliefs with religious elements important to the Japanese people as a whole. This will become more evident as we examine the festivals and prayers of the kakure Kirishitan.

Chapter
III

# Festivals and Prayers

# Introduction

Because of the ban on Christianity during the Tokugawa period, Japanese Christians, if they desired to observe special religious occasions, obviously had to camouflage the Christian element completely. Despite the long years of hiding and celebrating in secret, Christian roots were still found in many of the religious festivals and prayers continued by the kakure Kirishitan in the nineteenth century.

# Festivals

Observances varied from village to village, and it would therefore be impossible to discuss every festival practiced among the kakure Kirishitan. For this reason, only the major festivals in several villages of Ikitsuki will be discussed. (See tables 2 and 3.)

It was mentioned that in Kurosaki and the Gotō Islands, the Basutean calendar was used to determine the religious observances for the year, and at the weekly meetings the chōkata or the mizukata alerted the Kirishitan to the important upcoming religious dates. In Ikitsuki, where this custom was not followed, the dates of religious festivals were determined by the leaders at special gatherings.

One such gathering, the Dōyonakayori, was usually held in the sixth month, in the village of Yamada. (This village probably had the honor because it was the strategic center of Antonio Koteda's domain until 1557.) The decisions reached at this meeting were circulated to the other villages, which traditionally followed Yamada's lead. The meeting place, which was decided during the first part of the year, rotated among three *fure* (geographical areas) of Yamada: Baba, Honshoku, and Shoda.[1]

The Dōyonakayori was primarily concerned with the calculation of three movable feasts: the Jibiriya-sama (probably from *jubileo*), the Otobarai (autumn festival),

## Major Movable Festivals in Ikitsuki

| Lunar Month | Festival | Liturgical Calendar* |
|---|---|---|
| 1 | *Kazadome no gandate:* midmonth | |
| | *Hatsu oshikae:* first Sunday | *Lent:* forty-six days before Easter |
| | *Kanashimi no hairi:* between days 1 and 7 | |
| 2 | *Ohana nichiyōbi:* Sunday before Agiri | *Palm Sunday:* Sunday before Easter |
| | *Agiri:* forty-six days after Kanashimi | *Easter:* Sunday following full moon after vernal equinox |
| | *Osejo matsuri:* ten-day observance that coincides with Agiri | *Easter Octave, Corpus Christi* |
| 4 | *Dagokui (Mugifumi):* after wheat harvest | *Major litany:* Apr. 25 |
| 5 | *Tagitō:* after rice transplanting | *Minor litany:* thirty-six days after Easter |
| | *Mushi oi:* after rice transplanting | |
| 6 | *Dōyonakayori:* mid month | |
| 7 | *Jibiriya:* date determined each year | *Assumption of the Virgin Mary:* Aug. 15 |
| 9 | *Otobarai:* date determined each year | *All Souls Day:* Nov. 2 |
| 11 | *Gotanjō:* first Sunday after winter solstice | *Christmas:* Dec. 25 |
| 12 | *Ushi no gogandate:* end of month | |

*These dates are based on the solar calendar

## Table 2

and Gotanjō (Christmas). The date for Gotanjō was deter-mined by making it the first Sunday after the winter sol-stice, which, on the lunar calendar, placed it in the eleventh month. After the date of Gotanjō was decided, the other two feasts were calculated by *mikka sangari* (three days' delay). For example, if Gotanjō was the fif-teenth day, then Otobarai (which was always in the ninth month and undoubtedly refers to October) would be the eighteenth day, and Jibiriya-sama (which was always in the seventh month) would be the twenty-first day.[2]

The name *Jibiriya-sama* is thought to be from the Latin word *jubileo*. Both Tagita and Kataoka think this fes-tival might possibly have been related to the Assumption of the Mother of God into Heaven, celebrated on August 15 by the Catholic church. It also may have come to be associated with a plenary indulgence (full remission of the punishment for sin) that could be obtained on this day, and therefore the day was special for Christians.[3] A letter from a Jesuit, written in 1566, relates details of a big celebration in Hirado in August 1566, when a plenary indulgence was granted to the participants. The occasion was the dedication of a church building, which was placed under the protection of Mary, assumed into heaven, and the letter tells of the huge crowd that turned out for the occasion.[4]

The word could also be related to *vigilia* (vigil), the day before an important feastday, when Christian tradi-tion required prayer and fasting. When Tagita asked vari-ous people in Ikitsuki the meaning of the word *jibiriya*, he was told by kakure Kirishitan that it referred to the Bud-dhist Obon festival, which occurred about the same time. Those who were not kakure Kirishitan had no under-standing of the word. Therefore, he surmised that the kakure Kirishitan were exercising prudence by relating it to Buddhism in an attempt to hide its Kirishitan meaning.[5]

On the day that the kakure Kirishitan celebrated Jibiriya, the mideshi assembled in the tsumoto. In some areas, the believers assembled in the home of the mideshi. Finally there were areas where no assembly was held. In areas where a group did assemble, the celebration consisted of a simple recitation of prayers.[6]

Otobarai, in the ninth month, was celebrated as a festival to honor the dead. It was a special occasion when the kakure Kirishitan prayed for those who had died leaving no relatives behind to pray for them.[7] This observance could well have been related to the Christian feast of All Souls, observed on November 2 on the liturgical calendar; on this day, Christians pray for the souls who are suffering in purgatory because they failed to atone for their sins while still on earth. However, in Japanese folk religion one encounters the belief in *muenbotoke*, spirits with no surviving kin.

> These are the ghosts of those who have died with no surviving descendants to accord them the nourishing worship they require, who die childless and without kinsmen or lost and friendless in the course of a journey. They are, therefore, rootless, wandering, starved, desperate of hope for rest and peace. In their misery they will attack any passing stranger whose condition, through sickness or weakness, lays them open to spiritual possession. In many families, therefore, the custom still persists at the Bon festival of providing a separate altar for these homeless "hungry ghosts" whose sufferings may thus be temporarily assuaged.[8]

Whether it was the Christian feast of All Souls or the belief in muenbotoke that predominated in the minds of the kakure Kirishitan is impossible to determine. But it is entirely plausible that in their efforts to camouflage their Christian practice the kakure Kirishitan commemorated the feast of All Souls under the cloak of their belief in muenbotoke.

Festivals that were connected with the suffering, death, and resurrection of Christ were also movable feasts. Kanashimi no hairi (entering into sorrow), which corresponded to the season of Lent on the liturgical calendar, began between the first and seventh day of the first month, the Wednesday before the first Sunday designated as the opening of the season. On the Christian calendar, this was called Ash Wednesday, and almost always fell in the second month. The fortieth day after entering the season of sadness was called Ohana nichiyōbi (flower Sunday, or in Christian terms, Palm Sunday). The following Sunday was Agiri (rising, or Easter).[9] The celebration of Ohana nichiyōbi and Agiri coincided every other year with the Osejo matsuri, which will be discussed below. Generally, in these celebrations, there did not appear to be any understanding of the original meaning of the event commemorated.

Tagita suggests that because Kanashimi no hairi occurred in the first month on the lunar calendar, it was readily commemorated under guise of the traditional Japanese New Year's celebration. He believes that it was maintained in the religious life of the kakure Kirishitan because this was a slack period in the life of the farmer, when there was greater leisure to indulge in festival activities. It was during the forty-six days after Kanashimi no hairi that the kakure Kirishitan learned the prayers, and in some areas it was the only time that baptisms were allowed. This latter point is explained by the taboos connected with baptism, which were difficult for the sazukeyaku to observe during the busy farming months.[10]

Most of the observances connected with the New Year (or the season of Lent) occurred regularly on a fixed day, although the day varied from village to village, or were observed only in certain villages. In the first month there were several special gatherings. The first day, Hatsu mairi (first visit) was a holiday, and the kakure Kirishitan visited the tsumoto. The second (or third) day was called Osuwari (rice cakes), and on this day the year's rice in the form of rice cakes was offered to the nandogami. It was sprinkled with water to bless it; and on the following day,

called Mochi no hiraki (opening the rice cakes), the rice
was distributed among the mideshi present, who then
returned to their own area and divided the rice among
the compania, and then among the households that
belong to the tsumoto. This blessed rice could not be
given to any erenjamon (heretics).[11]

These festivals, except for the Christian prayers and
the fact that the offerings were made to the nandogami,
were quite similar to Japanese festivals commemorating
the New Year. Visits to a shrine or temple during the New
Year's celebration were customary as were visits to friends
and neighbors. The rice cakes (*mochi*) were "the most
important and sacred food at the New Year and other
festival days and ceremonies in Japan,"[12] and the distribution of the sacred rice cakes was common practice,
especially in rural Japan.

On the fifth and sixth days of the New Year, in Sakaime there were ceremonies for purifying the homes of the
kakure Kirishitan (*yabarai*) and for purifying the fields
(*nobarai*). For the purification of the homes, three officials
visited the kakure Kirishitan in their district. The highest
officials carried the holy water; the middle official, the
otempensia; and the lowest official, the ofuda.[13] They
sprinkled San Juan water on the foreheads of the resi-

*Otempensia and container of holy water*

dents. If a member of the household was absent, they sprinkled his or her kimono.[14] This festival in Sakaime was called Ojishi or Omyōdai.

This festival resembles the Gojinkin, which was held only in Moridakesaki. It was observed twice, on the fourth day of both the first and third months.[15] It also resembled the Nandogami no okazari (decoration of the nandogami) referred to by Kataoka Yakichi.[16] On this day, the nandogami was removed from its box, and special offerings were made. This was done at only one other time during the year, during the Osejo matsuri, which will be discussed below.

Before Nobarai, the ceremony of the purification of the fields, all the cattle were driven out of the field; then prayers were offered for the safety of people and animals; paper crosses were placed in hollow poles at the side of the fields; and finally, the cattle were allowed in again.[17] Tagita mentions a similar festival, Oyashiki-sama no matsuri, which was held only in Moridakesaki, celebrated on the twenty-ninth day of the eighth month.[18]

This festival dates back to the ancient court period (794–1185), when the ceremony was conducted at the court by the priestly Nakatomi family. Traditionally a purification ceremony was performed twice a year. Its purpose was to wash away physical and moral pollution, and it consisted of sprinkling water, reciting a ritual, and swinging the *nusa* (a small wooden or bamboo pole with a paper or cloth inserted in it).[19] The poles placed in the fields during the purification ceremonies of the kakure Kirishitan were probably related to the nusa, while the cross was clearly of Christian origin.

In Sakaime, toward the middle of the first month, a festival to stop the wind (Kazadome no gandate) was held. Believers gathered at the tsumoto and offered prayers for protection against destructive winds. In Yamada this festival was held during the sixth month, on the seventeenth, twenty-third, and twenty-ninth days. It

## Major Nonmovable Festivals in Jkitsuki

| Lunar Month | Festival | Liturgical Calendar* |
|---|---|---|
| 1 | day 1 *Hatsu mairi*<br>2 *Osuwari*<br>3 *Mochi no hiraki*<br>4 *Gojinkin*<br>5 *Yabarai*<br>6 *Nobarai* | *Epiphany:* Jan. 6 |
| 3 | day 3 *Hanahatsu nichi*<br>4 *Gojinkin* | *Major Litany:* Apr. 25 |
| 5 | day 5 *Kodomo no hi* | |
| 6 | day 17, 23, 29 *Kazadome no gandate*<br>18 *Kazadome no gandate*** | |
| 7 | day 13–15 *Obon* | |
| 8 | day 29 *Oyashiki sama* | |
| 10 | day 17, 23, 29 *Kazadome Ganjō ju no orei;* death anniversary of San Juan | |
| 12 | day 15–20 *Nenchū kinen matsuri* | |

*These dates based on the solar calendar
**According to Tagita (SJSK, 288)

# Table 3

was repeated in the tenth month on the same days and called Kazadome Ganjō ju no orei. In the sixth month, a group traveled to Nakae no shima to offer prayers. And in the tenth month, the kakure Kirishitan commemorated the death of San Juan.[20]

Osejo matsuri was one of the most important festivals in Sakaime. Tagita believes that the name came from the word *sejo* (worldly matters) and interprets it as a festival to pray for the prosperity of the house. It was also called Sangasho yori (the assembly of the three fure, or districts). The kakure Kirishitan celebrated this festival every other year during the third month, coinciding with the Agiri (Easter) celebration.[21]

This was the longest festival celebrated by the kakure Kirishitan, spanning a ten-day period. The first day, the leaders had to decide on the home that would house the assembled nandogami from the three fure. The second day, they sent out word as to which house had been chosen. The third day, two days before the actual celebration, was called *aramon torite* (collection), and contributions were accepted from each household and recorded. On the fourth day, *osuwarizuki*, large, triple rice cakes were prepared. On the fifth day, the festival day, the leaders and the people assembled and celebrated together with an abundance of food and drink. The following day, the leaders again gathered early in the morning, and after reciting prayers, they distributed rice to those present. On the seventh day they calculated the expenses incurred. During the following four days, the person chosen to guard the nandogami prayed along with the leaders. In the evenings, only the guards of the nandogami and the host remained in the house. The other members of the household slept in a room that was detached from the house. On the final day of the festival, the room used for the festival was returned to normal, the closet (*nando*) reverted back to a storeroom, and any materials borrowed for the occasion were returned.[22]

Tagita sees this festival as combining remembrances of the Easter celebrations and eucharistic processions held during the early Christian period. He sees its relationship to Easter both in terms of the length of the celebration and the time at which it was celebrated. In Catholicism, the Easter mystery was commemorated in the liturgy for a whole week following the feast, since it was considered the most important of the Christian mysteries. Tagita feels, therefore, that it is not coincidental that the Osejo matsuri was the longest of the festival celebrations among Ikitsuki Kirishitan.

The assembly of the nandogami during the celebration, he believes, was reminiscent of the eucharistic procession held on the feast of Corpus Christi, fifty-four days after Easter. On this day, the eucharist was placed in a decorative container (monstrance) and carried through the streets. The removal of the nandogami from their usual storage closet is likened to this procession.[23]

The kakure Kirishitan of Ikitsuki also celebrated many of the festivals that were commemorated in many other parts of Japan. Some examples are the Hanahatsu nichi (first flower, most commonly known as Doll's or Girl's Festival) on the third day of the third month; the Kodomo no hi (children's day, also known as Boy's Festival) on the fifth day of the fifth month; and the Obon matsuri, celebrated from the thirteenth to the fifteenth of the seventh month.[24]

Finally, there were several observances that related to the planting and harvesting of crops or to the need for rain. In the village of Sakaime, a festival called Dagokui was observed immediately after the wheat harvest. Dumplings were made from the wheat, and the people assembled in the compania to eat and to offer prayers of thanksgiving for the completion of the harvesting.[25]

The festival called Tagitō (field prayer) occurred usually during the fifth month, after the rice transplanting. The kakure Kirishitan placed sake and fish on a tray and offered prayers for the fertility of the five grains: wheat, rice, beans, and millet (*awa* and *kibi*). At this time, in Yamada, there was a festival called Mushi oi (driving out of insects), and it had the same purpose as the Tagitō, to pray for the fertility and safety of the field.[26]

Two other festivals held in Yamada were the Nenchū kinen matsuri (prayer festival during the year) and the

Amagai (prayer for rain). During the former, celebrated from the fifteenth to the twentieth of the twelfth month, the gobanyaku went to the various households and offered prayers for all persons and all things. The latter was obviously held only when there was a need for rain.[27]

Prayer offerings for a successful harvest became institutionalized in the early Catholic church in the celebration of the Rogation Days. The first, called the Major Litany, was celebrated on April 25; and the second, the Minor Litany, was commemorated three days before the Feast of the Ascension of Christ into Heaven, forty days after Easter. On the first Rogation Day, Christians made general prayer offerings; on the second, prayers for an abundant harvest. They often recited these prayers while walking in procession around their fields and farms. Tagita believes that the European missionaries undoubtedly tried to carry out these practices in Japan.[28]

For the Japanese, however, such rituals connected with planting and harvesting were familiar concepts. In describing common practices in Japanese agrarian communities, folklore specialist Hori Ichiro says:

> before seeding, several praying services for good crops are performed which are usually rich in magical elements; then come the rites for seeding; ceremonies for transplanting; praying for rain, for stopping storms or long rains, for frightening or driving away injurious birds or noxious insects; the offering of the new harvest and various customs accompanying it; and, finally, various harvest festivals for each family and community.[29]

Given the early missionaries' efforts to adapt themselves to Japanese culture, and the fact that their own European culture was predominantly agrarian, the importance of the harvest could not have escaped them. One can assume, therefore, that the Christian converts were encouraged to continue their prayers for the protection and abundance of their harvest but to address their prayers to the Christian God and to call on the mediating powers of the mother of God and the saints. And it appears that this is exactly what the kakure Kirishitan tried to do, for the festivals described by Hori parallel the festivals practiced by the kakure Kirishitan, and yet almost all the prayers they recited can be traced to the Catholic church.

Common to all the festivals described above was the necessity of food and drink (rice, fish, sake, and tea). The festivals provided the occasions for hard-working people to relax and enjoy one another's company, and the kakure Kirishitan therefore looked forward to them. Also common to all the festival celebrations was the recitation of prayers. We will now look at several examples of prayers that were recited by the kakure Kirishitan in Ikitsuki.

# Prayers

On Ikitsuki, there were about thirty different prayers that were recited in the course of religious observance. Most of these can be traced to prayers that the missionaries taught during the sixteenth and seventeenth centuries; others were devised by people of Ikitsuki themselves. Some of the prayers the Kirishitan recited were seemingly meaningless corruptions of the Latin versions. One such example is the Pater Noster (the Our Father). Below is a transcription in Roman letters of a tape recording made by Tagita in Yamada. It is followed by the standard Latin version.

> Pa-chiri no-chiri, ke-sense-rya, sanchimosen chimo, no-mentsu-wa-, asubereya-re-rentsu-wa i yao-randa estu-wa-. shikunise-rya-, ennente-rya-, Paanenna-no-chiriko-chiri, a-nonda no-bisu, o-rerebitano-bi sude bita no-bisu, shi-ku no, yot-suno, u-tsuno, jinmyo-chi . . . ribisu, tottorobisu, yo-nenna, shi-zu ka ni ententasha, yonen, sen-nebira-no, sanmaburo, anmezusu.

Latin version:

> Pater noster, qui es in caelis, sanctificetur nomen tuum; adveniat regnum tuum; fiat voluntas tua

sicut in caelo et in terra. Panem nostrum cotidi-
anum da nobis hodie; et dimitte nobis debita nos-
tra sicut et nos dimittimus debitoribus nostris; et
ne nos inducas in tentationem, sed libera nos a
malo. Amen.[30]

The relationship between the two prayers is quite evident, but the kakure Kirishitan version has no verbal
meaning.

Many of the prayers were translated into Japanese,
and the Kirishitan recited these as well. The first printed
text of prayers in Japanese appears to be the *Orashio no
Honyaku,* a combination prayerbook and catechism
probably first published in 1600.[31] Below is a comparison
of the Ikitsuki version of the Hail Mary and the version
found in the *Orashio no Honyaku.* First the Ikitsuki version:

Garassa michi michi tamaite, Mariya ni onrei o
nashi matsurite, onnaraji wa, onbito tomoni,
owashimasu. Yonin no naka ni oite mo, akete mo,
kaoyomijiki nari. Matagotainai no gomite
mashimasu. Deusu no on haa santa mariya, warera
wa kore ga saigo-nite, ware ra wa, akunin no tame,
tsutsu shin deta mō tamaiya. Anme-zusumariya.

And the Orashio version:

Garasa michi michi tamau Mariya ni onrei o nashi
matsuru go aruji wa ommi totomoni mashimasu.
Nyonin no naka ni o hite wakite goku wa
hōimishiki nari. Mata gotainai no omni nite
mashimasu zezusu wa tatsu toku mashimasu.
Deusu no on haha santa mariya. Ima mo warera ga
saigo ni mo warera akunin no tame ni tanomita-
mae. Amen.[32]

There is a greater similarity to the original when the
Kirishitan were memorizing prayers in their own lan-

guage. Those who have spent time with the kakure Kirishitan, however, agree that, by the nineteenth century, there was little or no understanding of the meaning of the prayers they recited.

The Ikitsuki Kirishitan, among their prayers, recited the eleven doctrines from the *Doctrina Christan*. The second of the eleven doctrines concerns the Trinity. Tagita says that the kakure Kirishitan were fairly accurate in translating this article, but it had no meaning for them. He found, rather, that the ability to recite the article was a matter of pride and gave the kakure Kirishitan a feeling of social superiority. He also found that they liked the mystery involved in reciting phrases, the meaning of which was obscure.[33]

The names of the seven sacraments were also recited as a chant. Baptism (Latin *Baptisma*) was pronounced *bautsurijima*, the last two syllables taken to mean island. (The Japanese word for island is *shima* or *jima*.) The other sacraments were recited as follows: *coerimansa* (confirmation), *yokanohitsuya* (eucharist), *tenbinsha* (penance), *yoshitarumansa* (extreme unction), *onre* (orders), *machirimo mia* (matrimony).[34] It is interesting to note here that the pronunciation for eucharist evolved to the meaning of eight days (*yōka*) and seven nights (*hitsuya*), and was sometimes written in Japanese kanji (the Japanese word for Chinese written characters) with that meaning.[35] Hence, this amounts to the recitation of seven words whose original meaning had been entirely lost.

But the recitation of meaningless syllables was not foreign to Japanese religious practice. Carmen Blacker says that among the Buddhist prayers, there were those whose

power resides in a succession of syllables from which all meaning has been lost. These are the *shingon* or mantras of esoteric Buddhism, and the longer *dhāranī*. In their original Sanskrit these sounds carried meaning. By the time they reached Japan in the eighth and ninth centuries the original Sanskrit sounds were distorted beyond recognition. They are now incomprehensible to all save the rare scholar of Buddhist Sanskrit who cares to trace the sounds back to their original source.[36]

The invocation of the names of deities also carries power. This was called *hōgō*. Blacker states, "The mere invocation of the divinity's name, several times repeated, is held to be power giving."[37] The kakure Kirishitan retained the practice of the recitation of litanies, where they recited the names of saints and titles of Christ and Mary taught by the early missionaries.

An example of a prayer that the kakure Kirishitan themselves devised is the "San Juan no uta" (St. John's Song), which was unique to the kakure Kirishitan of Ikitsuki and was recited only at the time of the Dōyon-akayori, in Yamada. There are three parts to the song, all of them centering on Nakae no shima. The three parts are translated as follows:

> In front, the spring
>> Behind, the high rocks
>>> In front and behind, only the sea water.

> This spring, the cherry blossoms fall
>> There are flowers which will bloom,
>>> Spring comes again.

> Let us go pray
>> Let us go pray at the temple of paradise
>>> It is a big temple, whether big or small it is in
>>> your heart.[38]

The first part of the song is a description of the island Nakae, as it would look to one sitting in a boat between Nakae and Ikitsuki or looking out from Ikitsuki. The spring or fountain refers to the spot where the holy water was miraculously obtained. The second part of the song commemorates the martyrdom of two Japanese Christians on Nakae no shima in 1622, Johannes Jiroyemon and Johannes Sakamoto Sayemon. The third stanza obviously looks toward the next life and rebirth in paradise.

*Nakae no shima*

Having examined the officials, the festivals, and the prayers of the kakure Kirishitan, one might still be puzzled as to what they actually believed. Because the kakure Kirishitan had to conceal their religious practice, their Christianity was passed along almost exclusively by oral tradition. Only one document has been discovered that gives a summary of how some kakure Kirishitan understood the Christian story. This is the *Tenchi hajimari no koto* (The Beginnings of Heaven and Earth).

Chapter
IV

# The Tenchi Hajimari
# No Koto

# Introduction

The *Tenchi hajimari no koto* (The Beginnings of Heaven and Earth), sometimes referred to as the bible of the kakure Kirishitan, came to light in the nineteenth century. It is first mentioned in a nineteenth-century work by a French priest, Francisque Marnas, in quoting a letter written by Bernard Petitjean, a French missionary, where Petitjean mentions that a baptizer, Domingo Fukahori Zenyemon, gave him a copy of a text that had been written from memory in 1822 or 1823. Petitjean says, "In transcribing it and translating it we notice errors here and there, but so far nothing substantial."[1] This version was lost, probably in the 1874 fire in Yokohama that destroyed the Catholic mission there.[2]

Tagita Kōya discovered eight versions of the *Tenchi hajimari no koto* in the 1930s, the earliest one dated 1827. It is not clear whether this early text was copied from another or written from memory. Since the complete Catholic Bible was not translated into Japanese before the country was closed in 1639, the Christian story was taught in summary form by the missionaries, from the creation story through the life, death, and resurrection of Christ, and the *Tenchi hajimari no koto* relates the story in this summary fashion. Of the eight versions of the text found by Tagita, five appear to have been written in the Nagasaki-Sotome area and three come from the Gotō

Islands. The one we will discuss here is the oldest version, the one Tagita considers the most beautiful.[3]

The text is interesting for several reasons. First, it contains major elements of Christian teaching: the creation story; the fall of the angels; the story of Adam and Eve; the salvation story, including the miraculous birth of the Son (Jesus) by the Virgin Mary and the death, resurrection, and ascension of the Son; and the end of the world. There can be no doubt that the story line is based on the teaching of the missionaries.

A second interesting aspect of the work is the inclusion of Buddhist terms and concepts and Japanese folklore. Finally, the changes made in the story shed light on the understanding of Christianity held by some Kirishitan in the nineteenth century. (Considering Petitjean's statement that he found no substantial errors, this text must differ remarkably from the text he received from Domingo Zenyemon.)

It is the last two points that we will investigate in more detail, but first, we will consider the content of the text.[4]

# Summary of the Tenchi

The story opens with Deusu, who possesses two hundred ranks and forty-two forms, creating the world. (The number of ranks and forms defines the quality of Deusu's character as they do the Buddha's in Buddhism.) He divides the light, and makes one sun-heaven, and then creates other heavens: Benbo (a hell, limbo?), Manbo, Oribete, Shidai, Godai, Happa, Oroha, Konsutanchino-hora, Koroteru, and Paraizo (Latin, *paradiso,* heaven). Mentioned next is the creation of the sun, moon, and stars, which may rank as a heaven, thus bringing the number of heavens to twelve.

Deusu then summons the *anjo* (angels), one being Jusuheru (Lucifer), who heads seven anjo, and who possesses one hundred ranks and thirty-two forms. Next Deusu creates earth, fire, water, wind, salt, and finally a man, Domeigasu-no-Adan (Adam). The seventh day is referred to as the first feast day, and the six preceding days of creation are given the Portuguese names for the days of the week. Woman is created next, Domeigasu-no-Ewa (Eve), and she and Adan are made a couple and sent to live in Koroteru (the origin of this word is not clear). Their children are called Chikoro and Tambo, a boy and a girl.

Meanwhile, Jusuheru deceives the anjo and encourages them to worship him. Some of them do, but when

Deusu appears, they fall down and worship him. This is called *konchirisan* (contrition). Deusu then tells them that they may not eat the forbidden fruit of the *masan* (Portuguese, apple). Once again, Jusuheru sets out and convinces Ewa that if she eats the fruit she will be like Deusu. She succumbs and offers it to Adan, who eats in turn, and then Deusu appears. Immediately Ewa and Adan recognize their mistake and begin to recite the *Salbehishina Orashio* (the Salve Regina, a prayer to Mary).

When Ewa and Adan beg Deusu for forgiveness, he tells them that they must do penance. Ewa, cast down to become a dog of the middle heaven, disappears. (Middle heaven may refer to limbo here; also the punishment shows influence of Buddhist reincarnation.) The fate of Adan is not mentioned. Ewa's children are told they will live on the earth below and do penance. Someday, Deusu tells them, he will show them the way to heaven. Jusuheru, in turn, is changed into a monster and sent out to the middle heaven as the god of thunder. All of the anjo who worshipped Jusuheru become *tengu* (goblins or devils) and are also sent to the middle heaven.

Meanwhile, down on earth, Ewa's children meet at a stone called Gojaku (serpentine), where Deusu had told them they would find something wonderful. The woman throws a needle and hits the man in the chest, drawing blood. He throws a comb, and they become man and wife, giving birth to many children.

As the people on the earth increase, food becomes scarce, and Deusu gives them seed rice. The yield is abundant even in winter. Next, the earth is troubled by ambition, greed, and selfishness. Even after Deusu casts these three evils to the bottom of the sea, greed and evil continue. Deusu tells a king called Pappa Maruji (pope and martyr) that when the eyes of the lion-dogs at the temple turn red the earth will be destroyed. Some of the children at the temple school, hearing the prophecy and finding it ridiculous, paint the eyes of the lion-dogs red. When Pappa Maruji sees this, he takes his six children and puts them on an ark that he had prepared, leaving the eldest son behind because he is lame; and the earth becomes a huge expanse of water. Those who drown in the flood go to Benbo (limbo?), and those on the ark, to an island called Ario. One of the lion-dogs rescues the lame son and carries him safely to Ario Island.

The people on Ario increase and, when they die, are sent to Benbo. Deusu asks an anjo how he can save these people, and the anjo says that he must divide himself. This he does, and Hiiriyo (Latin, *filio*, son) comes into existence. Deusu then sends the arikanjo (archangel) San Gaburiya (St. Gabriel) to earth. Next, the water official, San Juan (St. John), is conceived in the womb of Santa Izaberuna (St. Elizabeth).

In Roson (Luçon, the Philippines),[5] there is a king named Sanjenjejuusu (St. Joseph? [Tagita suggests that this name is derived from "Amen Jesus"]) and a maiden called Maruya. Maruya has received a message from heaven telling her that for her salvation she should live her entire life as a *birujin* (virgin). Meanwhile, the king of Roson decides on Maruya as his queen. She refuses and several miracles occur to prove to the king that she is special. The king dies pining with love for her.

The arikanjo San Gaburiya appears to Maruya and asks her to lend her body for the coming of the Lord. She agrees, and in the middle of the second month a butterfly flies into her mouth, and she conceives. After four months, Maruya sets out to visit Izaberuna, and they meet at the Abe river.[6] Izaberuna greets Maruya with the beginning of the Hail Mary, and Maruya recites part of the Our Father. They talk together for a while, and then both return home.

Maruya's family, seeing her condition, banish her from their home. She wanders until the eleventh month, when after fasting, she gives birth to Jejuusu, the Holy One, in a stable where she had taken shelter from the cold. The next day, the owner of the stable invites her to come into the house, and Maruya is given a hot bath. She suggests that the son of the household, suffering from the pox, also bathe in the same water, and he is cured of his illness.

On the eighth day, "because of worldly love, and desires and inconstancy,"[7] the Holy One receives *shi-rokushisan* (Portuguese, *circumcisão*, circumcision). After a short time, three kings receive a message from heaven and set out to find the Holy One. The three are Menchō, king of Turkey, Gasuparu, king of Mexico, and Bautozaru, king of France. They meet miraculously en route and follow the star as a guide to the land of Beren (Bethlehem). They stop to see the king of Beren, Yorōtetsu (Herod), who knows nothing of the birth of the Lord of Heaven. They invite Yorōtetsu to join them, but he refuses.

When the three kings arrive on the thirteenth day to find the Holy One, they are warned that they are in danger. And so, on their return, three bridges come down from heaven giving each a way to return to his native land.

Meanwhile, the king Yorōtetsu is seeking the Holy One because he fears the child will usurp his kingdom. He calls two of his retainers, Ponsha and Piroto (Pontius Pilate), who set out to kill all the young children of the realm. A miracle prevents them from catching up with the Holy One and Maruya.

As the Holy One and Maruya flee, they arrive at the river Bauchizumo (Portuguese, *batismo*, baptism) where they meet Juan, who baptizes the Holy One. The Holy One is now called Jusu Kirishito, and he wills the water of the river divided into more than forty thousand streams. It is now the water of salvation. On the fortieth day, the Lord goes to Taboro (Mt. Tabor). Deusu calls him to heaven for a visit and gives him a crown; then the Holy One returns to earth and on the fiftieth day goes into the chapel in Zezumaruya (Gethsemane). On this day he begins his learning from Sagaramento (Sacrament), who has come down from heaven for seven days and seven nights. The Lord continues his learning until age twelve.

The Holy One first shows his learning in a discussion with a Buddhist priest named Gakujuran (*gakushara*, plural form of Buddhist teacher) in a temple in Barando (basilica?). The two of them discuss the creation and afterlife, and, after much discussion, the twelve disciples of Gakujuran ask to be baptized, as do many visitors in the temple. The baptisms are presided over by the *konyesōru* (confessor). Gakujuran himself is convinced when his many scriptures are weighed alongside the one held by the Holy One and the latter is found to be heavier. He also receives baptism and then tells the Holy One to flee because Yorōtetsu is still seeking after him. So the Holy One and the twelve disciples leave for Rome, where they build a basilica called the Temple of Santa Ekirenjiya (Latin, *ecclesia*, church).

Yorōtetsu, continuing his search for the Holy One, orders all the children up to seven years of age to be killed, and the deaths number 44,444. The Holy One, hearing this, performs ascetic exercises at Zezemaruya. Deusu then informs the Holy One that he must suffer and die for the salvation of the children who died because of him. When the Holy One hears this, he falls down and sweats blood.

He returns to Rome and announces that he will be betrayed, identifying his betrayer as the one who swallows his rice with soup every morning. This is Judatsu (Judas), who informs Yorōtetsu that the one he seeks is a priest in the Temple of Santa Ekirenjiya in Rome.[8]

After the betrayal, Judatsu is returning to Rome with his reward money, when his nose and tongue grow long. He arrives weeping. After being rebuked by the other disciples, he goes out and hangs himself.

Yorōtetsu sends Ponsha Pirato (this time one person) with a large force to Rome. He captures the Holy One and presents him to Yorōtetsu, who has him whipped for causing the death of so many children and then sends him to Karuwaryu hill (Calvary) to be crucified. En route, carrying his cross, he meets a woman named Beronika

(Veronica), who comforts him, wiping the blood from his face. He leaves the image of his face on the cloth, and she presents it to the temple of Santa Ekirenjiya.

Two criminals are being crucified at the same time as the Holy One. One blames the Holy One for this; the other feels sorry for the Holy One. It is discovered that the latter was the same person who as a child had been cured of the pox by bathing in the miraculous water.

The torture continues day after day as the Holy One hangs on the cross, and the forty-six disciples do penance during this time. For this occasion the Holy One had composed the "Go-passho no orashio" (Passion Prayer). Because the forces of Yorōtetsu become weak every time they try to deliver the death blow, a blind man is found and offered a reward if he will do it. He agrees, and when the blood from the wound strikes his eyes, he is able to see. Because he rejoices in this and wishes he had done it sooner, he loses salvation and is immediately blinded again.

The Holy One is placed in a coffin and buried in the earth. On the day of Sabato (Sabbath) he sits on his coffin, and the disciples come to worship him. After ascending to visit Deusu, on the third day he sits at Deusu's right hand. Then he descends again to the temple of Ekirenjiya for the salvation of all people.

A man named Pappa (pope) is instructed by the Holy One for forty days. For ten days he preaches to the Abosutoro (Apostles), and on the fiftieth day he again ascends into heaven. Maruya is raised to heaven on the third day of the eighth month from a mountain called Oribete (Olivet). "Thus, in heaven, the mother is mediator, the Holy One is a savior. The parent Deusu is Paateru, the holy one is the Son, Hiiriyo, and the mother is Suberuto Santo (Holy Spirit). Deusu has become three. Although three, He is truly one."9

All of the children killed by Yorōtetsu are saved, along with those who helped the Holy One on earth. Maruya requests of Deusu that Jejuusu, the Holy One, be made her husband, and this is granted. Beronika is given the rank of Anesutera (Latin, *Agnus Dei*) to protect the world.

The officials of Paraizo are named San Migiri (St. Michael), who weighs sins; San Peitoro (St. Peter), the gate official; San Paburo (St. Paul), who examines the good and bad; San Juan, who inspects; Abosutoro (Apostles), who forgive; and Santosu (saints), who mediate between Deusu and those on earth.

The account ends with the prediction of the end of the world. It will eventually be destroyed by fire and wickedness, the devil working hard to lead people astray. At the end of the destruction, Deusu will reunite the *anima* (souls) of all people with their original bodies. Those anima who will continue to wander around forever are those whose bodies were cremated when they died or those whose bodies were eaten by another human being.

Then Deusu will come down and put all those who are saved on his right and those who are not saved or have not been baptized, on his left. Those on the right will go to Paraizo and receive the body of Buddha;* those on the left will go to a hell called Benbo, where they will stay forever.

---

*In Buddhist belief, achieving salvation means becoming one with the Buddha.

# Buddhist Influences

The Buddhist influences in the text are evident. First, the assigning of ranks to Deusu and Jusuheru clearly place them both in a position superior to Buddha. The complete character of the Buddha is said to have thirty-two marks or ranks.[10] Throughout Japanese history, Buddha has assumed many forms, dating back to the inclusion of Shintō deities as manifestations of the Buddha. Deusu in turn has forty-two forms, although these are not specified in the text.

In the process of creation, Deusu creates twelve heavens, and one of these is the sun-heaven. In Buddhism there is mention of twelve heavens, but the inclusion of a sun heaven might also refer to the sun goddess, Amaterasu, from Japanese Shintō mythology, from whom Japan's imperial line is said to descend. The names assigned to the other heavens created by Deusu do not appear to be related to Buddhist terms or, for that matter, to Japanese terms. Tagita suggests that *Benbo* may refer to limbo, *Oribete* to Olivet, *pappa* to pope, and *Konsutanchino* to Constantinople.[11] This seems entirely possible given the number of foreign words scattered throughout the text.

A pair of lion-dogs, chosen as messengers to warn the good king of the impending flood, were a common sight at the entrance to Shintō shrines and Buddhist temples in Japan. In the Gotō Islands, in Warabi, the kakure

Kirishitan had an image of Buddha that they viewed as the lion-dog that carried the lame son of the king over the waters to safety. He was called Korai-jizō (foreign jizō [a Buddhist guardian deity of children]).[12]

There are also similarities to the Buddhist belief in reincarnation: Jusuheru becomes a long-nosed goblin; Ewa, a dog of the middle heaven; Judatsu, after his betrayal, grows a long tongue and nose, thus becoming a goblin.

The most overt reference to Buddhism is, of course, the Holy One's discussion with the Buddhist priest in the temple, when he tries to prove that the Buddhist scriptures are worthless. This entire section of the text is reminiscent of the situation in the sixteenth and seventeenth centuries, when the missionaries endeavored to convince the bonzes that Christianity was the only true religion.

As mentioned earlier, one of the first things the missionaries did was to point out the errors in the religions of Japan. There were also instances during these years of Buddhist priests converting to Christianity. It is interesting to note that the Holy One, in his discussion with the priests, refers to Deusu as a Buddha.

Finally, in the story of the destruction of the world, the prediction that the dead who have been cremated or eaten by human beings will roam forever combines Buddhist and Christian teaching. Buddhists believe that those who die with no one to care for them will roam about and cause trouble. Christians in the sixteenth and seventeenth centuries considered cremation a violation of the sacredness of the body. And cannibalism, of course, has never been condoned by Christian or Buddhist teaching. According to the *Tenchi*, the baptized dead whose bodies have not been cremated or eaten will be given the body of Buddha in Paraizo.

The inclusion of Buddhist terms and concepts in the text can be explained readily by the fact that all Japanese had to register with a Buddhist temple during the Tokugawa period, and many of the kakure Kirishitan thus cloaked their Christian practice in Buddhist garb. Gradually, aspects of Buddhism could have been amalgamated into Christian beliefs, creating a new, meaningful belief. However, one should not discount the fact that the confusion of Buddhism and Christianity was a problem for the early missionaries, and the brevity of instruction afforded the converts did not augur well for a clear delineation of Buddhist and Christian doctrine. The Japanese Christians were exposed to concepts that were entirely foreign to their religious structures, and they naturally likened these new ideas to what they already knew. Also, the missionaries were encouraged to live, dress, and conduct themselves like Buddhist priests, and the Japanese who assisted them were identified by Buddhist names: dōjuku and kambō.

Whether Japanese Christians went underground with no clear distinction between Buddhism and Christianity or whether this developed during the long years of hiding is impossible to ascertain. But given the close relationship between religion and everyday life in Japan, one can argue that Christianity for many Japanese converts was just an addition to their religious life and that they placed it in their already rich tradition of beliefs, which contained elements of Shintō, Buddhism, Confucianism, and folk religion. For many, it was an important enough addition to risk persecution and death to maintain. But that they saw it as a religious belief that excluded their own religious traditions is not clear and indeed is difficult to accept.

# Influences of Japanese Folklore

One can detect influences of Japanese folklore in several places in the *Tenchi* text. First is the reference to the tengu, the long-nosed goblins. Only among the Kirishitan of Kurosaki is tengu synonymous with devil,[13] but the long-nosed goblins are popular figures in Japanese stories.

In the flood story, there are also elements of Oriental legends. An Oriental folk myth still popular in Shikoku, Kyūshū, and the Ryūkyū Islands tells of an island that is submerged into the sea because of the wickedness of the people. Only the good king and his family are spared because they are warned by a message from heaven: the eyes of the temple dogs turn red. As in the *Tenchi,* the children of the island ridicule the message.[14]

Mary's miraculous conception of the Holy One adds a detail not mentioned in the Christian story, namely, conception occurring when a butterfly flies into her mouth. As Tagita observes, legend says that Hideyoshi was conceived when the sun jumped into his mother's mouth.[15] This story could also have some connection with the Christian story, however, as the biblical text has the Angel Gabriel explaining Mary's miraculous conception as follows: "The Holy Spirit will come upon you and the power of the most high will overshadow you." (Luke 1:35) The traditional symbol of the Holy Spirit is a dove, and one can easily imagine this image evolving to that of a butterfly.

The text also offers its own explanation for the old Japanese custom of women shaving off their eyebrows and blackening their teeth. It is included in the flood scene. When the survivors of the flood arrive at Ario Island and decide to stay there to live, there are no rules or regulations governing husbands and wives. It was at this time, according to the text, that married women marked themselves by shaving off their eyebrows and blackening their teeth.[16]

Many details in the *Tenchi* are similar to those found in the *Kojiki* (Records of Ancient Matters) and the *Nihon shoki* (Chronicles of Japan), the oldest existing records of Japan, dating back to 712 and 720 respectively. Some examples are: the throwing of the comb and the needle, resulting in marriage; the seed rice given by Deusu that flourishes even in winter; and the bridge from heaven to conduct the kings miraculously and safely to their homelands. In the *Kojiki*, Susa-no-o (the brother of Amaterasu) protects the maiden he wants to marry by changing her into a close-toothed comb, which he inserts in his hair while he pursues the monster that is trying to kill her.[17] In the *Nihon shoki* there is mention of the Floating Bridge of Heaven.[18] And again in the *Kojiki*, Amaterasu tells her grandson that he and his descendants will rule over the "Reed-plain-1500-autumns-fair-rice-ear Land." (referring to Japan)[19] The point of these examples is not to imply a direct connection between the *Tenchi* and these early Japanese chronicles but rather that the details cited from the *Tenchi* may arise out of traditional Japanese myths.

Finally, the choice of the number 44,444 for the number of children killed by Yorōtetsu is significant in the Japanese language. One of the pronunciations for the number four in Japanese is "shi," which is also the pronunciation for the word "death." The repetition of the number four in the text may well have been meant to emphasize the wickedness of Yorōtetsu's deed. In the Christian Bible story, the number of children killed by Herod is not given.

# Christian Doctrine

The *Tenchi* text represents a unique example of a spontaneous, untutored "Japanization" of Christianity. In terms of Christian doctrine, it is enlightening to see which elements of the Christian story are retained and which are changed or omitted.

One of the most mysterious and difficult Christian beliefs, yet one of the first ideas introduced to the Japanese by the missionaries, is the doctrine of the Trinity. Christians believe there is one God but three distinct persons in that God: God the Father, God the Son, and God the Holy Spirit, all existing from eternity. The notion was retained in the text but with an understanding that differs significantly from the original teaching. Deusu, as he ponders how to rid the earth of greed and other evils, takes the suggestion of the anjo and divides himself, thereby creating a messenger called Hiiriyo (son) to go to earth to help the people. Toward the end of the text, Maruya is referred to as the Santo Spirito. Thus the three persons of the Trinity are not thought to exist from all eternity, and Maruya's assuming the person of the Holy Spirit is contrary to Christian doctrine. Because the kakure Kirishitan memorized many of their beliefs in the early days of Christianity, they passed on correctly the words of this mystery, but they either never grasped the significance of it or lost it over the long years of hiding.

A second doctrinal element included in the text but foreign to the Christian story is Maruya's request to Deusu that she be given the Holy One as her husband after she has been raised up to Paraizo. She asks this because she has lived out her entire life on earth as a biru-jin (virgin) and the Holy One has died for love of her. This has no counterpart in biblical theology. It may have some relationship to terminology used in the Catholic church, which refers to both male and female religious as spouses of Christ; also, there are references to Christ as the bridegroom and the church as the bride. The missionaries were undoubtedly called upon to explain their unmarried status, and this could account for its inclusion in the text in regard to Maruya.

The reason for the Holy One's suffering and death raises another doctrinal question. In the earlier portion of the text, Deusu tells the Holy One that he must suffer and die because of all the children who were massacred by Yorōtetsu, and Yorōtetsu himself gives that as his reason for the condemnation of the Holy One. In Christian teaching, Jesus subjects himself freely to crucifixion and death to atone for the sins of all humankind. Toward the end of the *Tenchi*, we learn that all those who helped the Holy One (i.e., believed in him?) while on earth will ultimately be saved. But nowhere does the text state that this salvation is a result of the Holy One's suffering and death.

This difference in interpretation seems readily understandable. The notion of sin does not exist in Japanese religious belief. Even though the missionaries were able to convince the Japanese converts that they must confess and be sorry for any thoughts and actions that went against Christian teaching, it was undoubtedly quite difficult to explain that a god would suffer such abject humiliation for the sins of all humankind. It would indeed be more reasonable and understandable to assume that he died to atone for the deaths of thousands of innocent children who died as a result of a search for the Holy One. Thus, the Kirishitan retained the notion that the

Holy One had the power to save people but did not relate this to his suffering and death.

One mystery central to Christian mystery entirely omitted in the text is the eucharist, which rivals the Trinity for difficulty. In Catholic teaching, Jesus Christ instituted the eucharist the night before he died (see Luke 22:14–20) and empowered his apostles to carry it on. The eucharist is believed to be the body and blood of Christ under the form of bread and wine. According to church teaching, only ordained priests have the power to change bread and wine into the body and blood of Christ in the form of bread and wine. There were no priests during the Tokugawa period, and the Christians therefore had no access to this sacrament. Nor, apparently, did they ever empower their own officials to perform this kind of liturgy. Over time, the notion of the eucharist completely disappeared as a sacrament to be received by the believer; like the Trinity, perhaps it was never fully understood.

We have seen throughout these chapters that the officials and many of the religious practices and prayers of the kakure Kirishitan can be traced to the teachings of the early missionaries. At the same time, the kakure Kirishitan came into the nineteenth century with very little understanding of the doctrines of the Catholic church as these were originally taught to their ancestors. In order to come to a better understanding of the religion practiced by the kakure Kirishitan, we must examine the degree of continuity between the kakure Kirishitan practices of the nineteenth century and those of their sixteenth- and seventeenth-century ancestors; we must attempt to see the kakure Kirishitan in the broader context of the traditional Japanese approach to religious belief. We will be in a better position to deal with these questions, however, if we first look at the encounter between the kakure Kirishitan and nineteenth-century Roman Catholicism.

Chapter
V

# The Return of the Missionaries

# historical Background

The Catholic church had never given up hope of returning one day to Japan. Francis Xavier had written to his
Jesuit brothers in Goa in 1549:

> By the experiences which we have of this land of
> Japan, I can inform you thereof as follows. Firstly,
> the people whom we have met so far are the best
> who have yet been discovered, and it seems to me
> that we shall never find among heathens another
> race to equal the Japanese.[1]

Not only was Xavier's statement about the Japanese
encouraging, but the many stories of the courage with
which the Japanese Christians had faced execution for
their beliefs attested to their steadfastness and fidelity. In
1831, the Society for the Propagation of the Faith, in
Rome, took the first step toward return to Japan. It
entrusted the conversion of Japan and Korea to the
Société des Missions-Etrangères de Paris (Paris Foreign
Mission Society—M.E.P.). This group was founded in 1660
for the exclusive purpose of training priests for missionary work. Remembering the disputes among the various
missionary groups in Japan and China in the seventeenth
and eighteenth centuries, the M.E.P. group asked and

obtained permission from the Propagation of the Faith to be the only Roman Catholic priests in Japan. With no access to Japan at this time, French missionaries took up residence on the Ryūkyū Islands in 1844, began learning Japanese ways and the Japanese language, and made several unsuccessful attempts to reach Japan proper.[2]

The conclusion of the U.S.–Japan Treaty of Friendship (the Kanagawa Treaty) in 1854 encouraged the missionaries considerably since they believed a treaty with France would follow quickly. They increased their efforts at language study and prepared to re-enter this land where much blood had been spilled in the name of religion. Representatives of the French government were equally enthusiastic, eager to open new trade relations and extend the laissez-faire principle of economics to Japan. A commercial treaty between France and Japan was signed on October 9, 1858, and ratified on September 22, 1859. (The U.S.–Japan Treaty of Amity and Commerce was concluded in July 1858.)

The treaty states in Article IV that French subjects would have the right to practice their religion freely and would be allowed, on their territory, to erect those edifices deemed necessary to their religion, such as churches, chapels, and cemeteries. The Japanese, in turn, promised to abolish all practices that were injurious to Christianity.[3] But the Edict of 1614, which made it a crime for a Japanese to practice Christianity, remained in force.[4] Clearly, the missionaries would be allowed to serve the needs of the foreign Catholic population only.

The first Catholic missionary to enter Japan legally since the proscription of Christianity was Prudence S. Girard, who came to Edo (Tokyo) with the French Consul-General, M. Duchesne de Bellecourt, on September 6, 1859, as the consul's interpreter. Following him two months later came Eugene E. Mermet de Cachon, who installed himself at Hakodate and opened a small chapel in 1860 and later a dispensary and a French language school. Pierre Mounicou completed the construction of a church in Yokohama in 1861, and in 1865 a third church was dedicated on the Oura slope in the French concession under the direction of Bernard Petitjean and Joseph-Marie Laucaigne.[5]

Not being allowed to go about and preach to the Japanese people, the missionaries hoped these public displays of Christianity would bring the Japanese to them. A statement made in connection with the dedication of the Oura church tells much about the attitude of the Catholic church in this second period of Japanese Christianity:

> Doesn't the presence of our separated brothers [here referring to Japanese in general] at the inauguration of a Catholic church in a land which up to now has rebelled against European influence seem like homage rendered to Catholic civilization, alone capable of founding lasting establishments and of civilizing nations?[6]

Such a lofty statement reflects the defensive position that the church was forced to assume in the West at this time. Pius IX's encyclical *Quanta Cura* (September 1864) attacks the major intellectual trends of the day, such as rationalism, salvation outside the Catholic church, separation of church and state, political liberalism, and the idea of progress.[7]

The encyclical makes three "solemn affirmations: (1) the absolute independence of the Church against any civil authority; (2) her sacred right to train consciences, particularly those of the young; (3) the plentitude of papal authority, even in the spheres 'which do not concern faith and morals.'"[8] The *Syllabus of Errors* published along with the encyclical attacked current doctrines such as naturalism, pantheism, indifferentism, and utilitarianism and ends with the stinging statement, "If anyone thinks that the Roman Pontiff can and should reconcile himself and come to terms with progress, with liberalism and with modern civilization, let him be anathema."[9]

Many have referred to these documents as declarations of war against the nineteenth century, and indeed, they paved the way for a Catholicism increasingly isolated from the dominant trends of the larger society for the next century. At the same time, it was the secular European and American society that initially caught the fancy of the Japanese as they struggled to gain an equal footing with the Western world.

The missionaries had to contend not only with the absolute stance of the church expressed above but also with the stringent guidelines developed during the eighteenth century in answer to the famous Rites Controversy in China. The dispute focused on whether it was a compromise of Roman Catholicism to use Chinese words to express Christian concepts, to relate Catholicism to Confucianism, and to allow Chinese converts to perform rites in honor of Confucius and their ancestors. The Jesuits in China, led by Matteo Ricci, believed that these practices in no way compromised the Catholic faith, and in the spirit of Francis Xavier and Alexandro Valignano they tried to accommodate themselves to the cultural life of the Chinese. Franciscan and Dominican missionaries, however, took the other side in the argument and were horrified at what the Jesuits were doing. The controversy raged on, and finally a series of papal statements made in 1704, 1715, and 1742 forbade the missionaries to allow the Chinese converts to continue their practice of their own rites. Interestingly, members of the Société des Missions-Etrangères de Paris were also in China at that time, and they sided with the Dominicans and the Franciscans. The last decree, issued in 1742, was the clearest condemnation of the Jesuit practices in China and threatened the most severe sanctions for any violators.

In China, as in Japan, rites honoring ancestors and festivals related to farming and general prosperity are part of the everyday cultural life of the people. One might therefore say that the Rites Controversy prepared Catholic missionaries to war against the East Asian society by making it mandatory to forbid Catholic converts to participate in "pagan" observances.

This background provides the setting for the reacquaintance of Catholic missionaries with the kakure Kirishitan, which began on March 17, 1865, at the Oura church in Nagasaki, when a group of Japanese confronted Bernard Petitjean in the new church and informed him, "The heart of all of us here is the same as yours. . . . We are from Urakami and almost everyone there has the same heart as us."[10] Petitjean recounts that his doubts about the meaning of their words were erased when one of the women asked him where she might find the statue of "Santa Maria" ("Santa Maria no gozō wa doko"?).[11]

This part of the story is a familiar one, and has been told and retold countless times. The knowledge that the church had endured through the long years of persecution and proscription gave the missionaries a place to start—a dream they had half-heartedly considered but never fully expected to materialize. Of immediate concern was the discovery of all of the descendants of Japan's first Christians, and the search led them to the Nagasaki area and subsequently to Amakusa, Kurosaki, the Gotō Islands, Ikitsuki, and Hirado.

As the missionaries searched for the Christian remnant in Japan, they discovered descendants of Japan's first Christians who preferred not to be discovered and who preferred not to admit their Christian heritage. Nor did these Christians welcome being told that the beliefs they held, the prayers they recited, the baptisms they performed were not in accord with the nineteenth-century teachings of the Catholic church.

Let us now turn to the work of the French missionaries as they attempted to revive Catholicism in nineteenth-century Japan.

# Mission Activity

The French missionaries encountered many of the same problems as their predecessors: the language barrier, persecutions, what to teach, and adaptation. They faced two additional problems, however. First, the Catholic religion was now not the only form of Christianity in Japan. Protestant missionaries arrived in Japan along with representatives of their governments and began a successful mission activity that attracted a number of former samurai. Thus the Catholic missionaries had to struggle against Christian sects as well as against Japanese Buddhism and Shintō. Second, the discovery of a Christian remnant in Japan demanded immediate attention, and the fact that approximately one half of this remnant did not welcome the missionaries' return baffled them and consumed much time and energy. Their reactions toward the kakure Kirishitan provide an insight into the confrontation between a rigid nineteenth-century Catholicism and a set of religious practices clearly stemming from Catholicism but so altered as to make them unacceptable to the French missionaries.

Let us look at the problems faced by the nineteenth-century missionaries and the way they dealt with each of them.

# Language

As mentioned above, the French missionaries spent some time in the Ryūkyū Islands prior to the re-opening of Japan in order to acquaint themselves with the Japanese mores and language. Early observations made by the missionaries, however, indicate that language continued to be a problem.

Jules-Alfred Renaut, a young, enthusiastic missionary, arrived in Japan in early 1875 and kept a rather sketchy diary of his impressions during his first years there.[12] His observations are interesting, particularly those dealing with the language problem. For example, on July 7, 1875, he writes, his superior suggested that Renaut begin his study of Chinese characters because in talking to pagans one must appear educated. Renaut began the study on July 12. On July 25, he tells his diary that he has decided he must begin speaking directly to the pagans in the few Japanese phrases he knows. That he kept his resolve is evident, as his subsequent diary entries record encounters and conversations with pagans. And he notes that on August 25 he gave his first catechism lesson to two former samurai.

Another missionary, Michel Sauret, who arrived in Japan in 1879, comments on his language problem saying, "It is necessary to make unheard of contortions with the tongue in order to pronounce Japanese, learning to speak as a child of two or three; it takes a great deal to reduce oneself to babbling at the age of 30!"[13]

Language also proved a problem in a controversy that developed among the missionaries over what words to use in writing a catechism for use among the Japanese interested in Catholicism. The missionaries in the Nagasaki area, who were in contact with Japan's Christian descendants, thought it best to keep the Latin-Portuguese vocabulary that had been used since Japan's Christian beginnings. Petitjean and Laucaigne took this stance, arguing that this terminology was all these Christians knew and that it had been passed on through seven generations.[14]

The missionaries in Yokohama, Prudence Girard and Peter Mounicou, who wanted to use the Chinese characters then in vogue among missionaries in China, had an equally valid argument. They were working with peasants who had had no contact with Christianity, and the Portuguese-Latin terminology would have been entirely meaningless to them. Girard and Mounicou therefore wrote their own catechism, which was actually an adaptation of a catechism being used by missionaries in China, and Girard, as superior of the mission, circulated his work for use throughout Japan. Nagasaki-area missionaries responded with a complaint that these gentlemen "dreamed of the conversion of masses of peasants, and they sacrificed our Christians."[15]

Petitjean kept the catechism sent from Yokohama under lock and key and wrote to the office of the Propagation of the Faith for instructions. While awaiting word from Rome, he used the catechism that he and Laucaigne had prepared.[16]

The problem was solved rather fortuitously when Petitjean was elevated to the episcopate on June 22, 1866, and replaced Girard as the vicar apostolic in Japan.[17]

# Persecutions

In 1865, after word had spread among Japan's Christian descendants that the bateren had returned, Christians came to the priests and informed them of areas where there were believing Christians. Both priests and Christians defied government orders by attempting clandestine meetings, and in 1868, after the fall of the Tokugawa Bakufu, the new Meiji government attempted once again to enforce the ban against Christianity. Japanese Christians thus endured renewed persecutions from 1869 to 1873. Approximately four thousand Christians on Kyūshū were exiled to various parts of

Japan, some as far northwest as Nagoya. Although it appears that no Christians were executed, many died in the hardships of leaving home, friends, and belongings; and those that did return suffered great losses both financially and in social status. There was no action taken against the missionaries.

Representatives of foreign governments present in Japan at the time issued statements of protest to the Japanese, and in 1873 the Meiji leaders ordered anti-Christian signboards to be removed. Although the ban on Christianity was not officially rescinded at this time, overt persecution ceased for the most part and Christian proselytizing began in earnest.[18]

The missionary accounts after 1873 speak of trouble with the authorities because of religion, but only rarely. For example, in 1879 Petitjean mentions that the Christians in Amakusa were harassed because of their Christian burials.[19] As late as 1882 a local official in the prefecture of Bingo informed the residents of his locality that Christianity was still forbidden. When confronted by Japanese catechists, the official asked forgiveness and told the people that he did not know that the law was no longer being enforced.[20] In 1887, in Urakami, Christian converts were threatened with a fine.[21] One author feels that the attitude of the Japanese government toward Christianity was merely one of tacit approval and "the toleration of Christianity was due primarily to the government leaders' concession to the pressures from the Western powers."[22] Nevertheless, from 1873 on, Christians were free to confess their faith with little or no government harassment.

## Teachings

Because there had been no changes in the basic church doctrine taught by the missionaries since the seventeenth century, the teachings of the nineteenth-century missionaries cover the same area as the teachings offered to the

first Christians. The book printed in the Kirishitan terminology by Petitjean resembles the *Doctrina Christan* used
in the first Christian period. It consists of four books: the
origin of the Christian religion; the Creed; the Ten
Commandments, the Precepts of the Church, the seven
sources of sin; and the works of mercy, grace, and prayer;
and the sacraments.[23]

The text prepared by Mounicou, patterned after the
catechism in use by the church in China at the time,
begins with three paragraphs: the creation of heaven and
earth, original sin, and a summary of Christian doctrine. Then it is divided into four chapters: the Apostles'
Creed, prayer, the Ten Commandments, and the seven
sacraments.[24]

The missionaries' first aim was to win back the
Christian descendants, most of them common people, to
an orthodox practice of Roman Catholicism. Many of
these Christians' ancestors had found it necessary to flee
to secluded areas, or to areas not easily accessible, and by
the nineteenth century the great majority of Kirishitan
were poor, uneducated people making their living by
farming and fishing.

The nineteenth-century Catholic missionary activity,
therefore, was somewhat different from that of the sixteenth and seventeenth centuries, when Jesuits worked
from the elite of society down to the commoners. The
French missionaries began with the common people who
already had some notions of Christianity, while Protestants at the same time were making great headway
among the former samurai and upper echelons of Japanese society. Conspicuous by their absence during this
second period of Japanese Catholicism were the intellectual disputes between the missionaries and the Buddhist
priests, the conversions of Japan's elite, and the mass conversions. The relative success of Protestantism in Japan
might well be explained by the fact that Protestant
churches welcomed and embraced nineteenth-century
values while the Catholic church rejected them.

During the years after 1865, the Catholic missionaries, like their predecessors, relied heavily on the services of interpreters and catechists; but with the advances in printing and transportation, ready access to printed materials on Catholicism allowed for a more thorough indoctrination of the catechists and of those converts who were able to read. By 1880, there were eighty churches and chapels, three seminaries, sixty-seven schools and orphanages conducted by the French priests, and several orders of religious women, also from France.[25]

## Adaptation

Somewhat overlapping the discussion of teachings is the consideration of the French missionaries' attempts to adapt themselves to Japanese culture. Two important points must be emphasized here. The first is the effects of the Rites Controversy and the defensive posture of the Catholic church in the nineteenth century, which led to a stance of rigid authoritarianism. Since France was considered the eldest daughter of the church and the defender of Catholicism in the Western world, French missionaries reflected the church in her most orthodox posture. One would therefore not expect to see great creativity in adapting Catholicism to Japanese culture. Second, Japan's new Meiji government was eager to learn from the West and, up to the late 1880s, many Japanese were enamored of Western architecture, dress, food, and entertainment. With Japan striving so hard to become like the West, one can assume that Westerners were not terribly pressured to accommodate themselves to things Japanese.

With these points in mind, it becomes clear that the French missionaries saw little reason to strive toward adaptation. The only examples that could be found will illustrate that this was not a matter of major concern.

The first and most obvious example is the missionaries' realization that they must learn the Japanese language. A second example is Petitjean's insistence on continuing to use the Kirishitan style of writing in the catechism. And a third, from Renaut's diary (August 19, 1875), records that Renaut's superior advised him, when speaking to pagans, not to speak of the more painful or difficult religious obligations in becoming Catholic until the pagan had shown some interest in baptism. The areas to be avoided were the necessity of burning the *kamidana* (Shintō household altar), and the elimination of extra-marital sexual relations and adultery. The latter two examples were but temporary measures to ease the convert's entrance into Catholicism. They do not reflect a deep sympathy for or understanding of Japanese culture.

Because the French missionaries mirrored their society and their church, they were far less flexible and accommodating than the early missionaries. One should therefore not be surprised to find that they were not inclined to compromise with or accept the kakure Kirishitan beliefs and practices.

# Attitudes of the Missionaries toward the Kakure Kirishitan

The French missionaries refer to the kakure Kirishitan throughout their accounts as *les séparés* (the separated). Among the earliest references made to the kakure Kirishitan are those found in Renaut's diary. He gives the impression that while the missionaries were advised to move slowly with the pagans in explaining Christian teachings, with the kakure Kirishitan they moved right in, demanding that they get rid of their kamidana, obey the commandments, correct errors in their baptismal formulas, repair their marital relations—in general, become Catholic according to church law. Because they were descendants of Japan's first Christians and called themselves Kirishitan, they were given no leeway in their practices. Renaut refers to them in one entry as "bad Catholics." (August 11, 1875)

In August 1875, Renaut records that his superior has warned him not to go to the home of the kakure Kirishitan unless they summon him. If, by mistake, he finds himself in one of their homes, he is to leave unless specifically invited to remain. Over the next several months, Japanese Catholics begin revealing some of the locations of the kakure Kirishitan, and Renaut, along with his Japanese catechist, began seeking them out, armed with a list of locations. He does not mention why he begins going against the advice of his superior. On November 29, 1876, one of the catechists had a rather unpleasant encounter with a Christian who told him it was wrong to ask for the location of the kakure Kirishitan. The catechist went back to Renaut's superior and begged that Renaut be prevented from visiting the kakure Kirishitan unless he was certain that they wanted him. Renaut does not go into detail on this problem, but the tensions between the kakure Kirishitan and the returned Catholics (the kakure Kirishitan who joined the missionaries) are obvious.

The missionaries, in their reports sent back to their Paris headquarters, shed additional light on their early contacts with the kakure Kirishitan. One of the most perplexing questions for the priests to answer was why these people from Christian families would not return to the church. In trying to explain the reasons behind the reluctance of the kakure Kirishitan, the missionaries mention fear the most often.[26] During the early years of their mission, they seemed to understand this fear and were sympathetic. But as time went on, they began to view the fear of the kakure Kirishitan in a more hardnosed fashion. Any time fear is mentioned after about 1886, the writer hastens to add that it is unfounded or imaginary.

A second reason cited often by the missionaries for the difficulties in winning the kakure Kirishitan back is the influence exerted by prominent people in the local area or the influence of the baptizers, those men who by heredity or election execute a priestly function for the kakure Kirishitan.[27] Coupled with the above reason, concern about reputation, self-interest, and lack of courage are often mentioned, implying that the kakure Kirishitan are following the path of least resistance.

In Petitjean's first encounters with Japan's Christian remnant he describes in a general way their religious structures. He recounts that in most of the villages there are two officials. The first, in charge of prayer, is responsible for presiding over the Sunday religious exercises; it is he who visits the dying, suggesting that they make an act of contrition and recommend their souls to heaven. The second is the baptizer, who holds the office for ten years; he has a disciple who is elected to succeed him.

Petitjean's description of the kakure Kirishitan practices is more revealing. He indicates that there were some problems with the administration of baptism and with marital relationships that had been contracted during the hidden period. His first concern was baptism, and he worried about the instances of its invalid administration. Some of the questions he raised were: Are the words used correct? Even if correct, were the words pronounced before or after the pouring of the baptismal water rather than while reciting the formula? Was the amount of water used so small that it was insufficient to run over the head of the newly baptized? He says that some baptizers were content to immerse a piece of paper in water and apply it to the candidate's head. Others poured the water but said no words. Still others said the words over the water and then poured it or had the candidate drink it.[28]

This first problem had a ready solution. The missionaries simply demanded that the Kirishitan be rebaptized conditionally in the orthodox manner. But such a rigid stance on the part of the church presented major problems for the Japanese involved. The order constituted a loss of face for the baptizer. Submitting himself and all those whom he had baptized to a "correct" baptism was a public admission that he had erred and that he had, in effect, deceived his followers. For both the baptizer and the baptized, to admit that they were in error was tantamount to betraying what they had learned from their ancestors. Anyone possessing even a minimal understanding of the importance attached to saving face in Japan and of the deep reverence Japanese have for their ancestors can imagine the difficulties involved in the missionary directive.

The second problem, that of marriages, Petitjean found no less troublesome. Marriage consisted, he said, of a festive gathering. It was neither a civil nor a religious affair, and the contract could be broken with the consent of the parties involved. This was not acceptable to the church. The problem of what to do when Japanese Christians had already had children by a second marriage was not solved by Petitjean.[29]

The question was further complicated because the kakure Kirishitan had maintained the belief that marriage with one not of the Kirishitan religion was forbidden. There was, therefore, a high proportion of marriages between persons related by blood or by marriage.[30] Also, because the kakure Kirishitan had to practice their religion in secret, to marry outside the religion meant either detection or the necessity of giving up their religious practice.

In 1878, the hope of winning the kakure Kirishitan back to Catholicism seemed a difficult task indeed. One missionary complained that they were further away from conversion than the pagans.[31] And as the missionaries became more aware of kakure Kirishitan practices, they became all the more baffled. Writing to his parents in 1881, M. Sauret says that the kakure Kirishitan of Urakami did not even understand the prayers and ritual they used. He says he saw a magnificent Shintō temple (*temple Chintoïste*) in Hirado where there was still a rosary confraternity. The group met monthly to decide on the mystery for meditation. And in Ikitsuki, he found that they had preserved the Salve Regina, a prayer to the mother of God, and the psalm Miserere in Latin. The latter, he found, was chanted on almost the same tone as in the West.[32] Jules Alphonse Cousin, after listening to the recitation of these and other prayers one entire evening in Ikitsuki, laments:

> these poor people continue to sing, to baptize, to ask God's pardon for their sins, and their homes are decorated with idols, and they go to the Buddhist Monasteries (*Bonzeries*) out of fear of

persecution!!! The ways of God are incomprehensible! and what torment to think that these souls so close to heaven, may fall into hell.[33]

In 1887, the first mention is made by the missionaries of the kakure Kirishitan themselves claiming that the religion being taught by the French is not their religion—this from Japanese living in the Gotō Islands.[34] And a group of Christians from Ono, in the Sotome area, criticizes the missionaries for not allowing for special days on which to honor Basutean, a saint for the kakure Kirishitan.[35]

At the same time that the kakure Kirishitan were complaining about their teachings, the missionaries found Protestant proselytizing had become a trial in their mission efforts. Michel Sauret, writing in 1887, says:

> If we Catholics were alone in Japan our position would be beautiful, however, the Japanese, seeing the divisions which exist between Catholics, Protestants and Russians, figure that the Christian religion is the same thing as Buddhism, which is to say it is divided into a number of sects and it is impossible to discover which is the true one. As they are superficial in all they do, they do not take the trouble to discover the difference.[36]

One catches here, in Sauret's last statement, the sense of superiority often displayed by the Western missionaries. In the report the following year, this same attitude is reflected when one writer compares the kakure Kirishitan to the Jews who recite prophecies that condemn them, without even trying to understand.[37] The missionaries complain that it takes impending death or the desire to marry a Catholic to move the kakure Kirishitan to baptism.

By 1888–89, conversions among the kakure Kirishitan had virtually ceased.[38] But the missionaries had not given up trying to get at the root of the kakure Kirishitan's continued recalcitrance. Petitjean had written in 1880, in reference to Ikitsuki, "It's strange, it is the women who, on this island, place obstacles in the way of a return to the religion."[39] Unfortunately, he did not elaborate on the point. But Cousin does in 1888; also writing about the island of Ikitsuki, he says:

> They are stopped [from conversion] by the imaginary fear of new persecution, by the trouble caused them by certain pagans in the area, by human respect and especially by the women. Actually, fearing the too great loquacity of the weaker sex, these men, who up to 1873, hid their observance of certain Christian practices, like meeting to recite prayers or doctrinal matters, completely eliminated the women from their assemblies, and ended by removing from them all means of learning the Christian traditions. With this system, the women soon became zealous pagans and now it is they who constitute the greatest obstacle to the conversion of Ikitsuki Island.[40]

One can sense the growing discouragement among the missionaries, and as the years pass it is almost as if they are grasping at straws in trying to analyze their failure among the kakure Kirishitan.

Cousin, writing in 1891, talks first of fear and ignorance as the reasons for the continuing separation but goes on to place some blame back in Japan's first Christian period. He says:

> The former missionaries of Japan . . . belonged to different religious families. There were Jesuits, Franciscans, Augustinians and Dominicans. These orders did not work in one specific area to the exclusion of other areas; they all worked in the same field, according to their interests and

circumstances. One finds, therefore, in the same city, the same hamlet, Catholics living side by side but frequenting different churches . . . dividing them from one another on the subject of particular devotions and practices. This was the downfall of this newly born Church, which did not find within itself, at the time of persecution, the unity and cohesion which was necessary in order to resist.[41]

This is an obvious oversimplification as becomes evident in any reading on the period of persecution.[42] Converts, totaling probably no more than three hundred thousand, would have been incapable of withstanding the increasing power of the new Tokugawa shogunate. As C. R. Boxer points out:

The ingrained habit of obedience to feudal superiors was doubtless one reason for the docility which the majority displayed; for the Christians perhaps felt that the mere profession of Christianity in defiance of the Shogunal edicts was something unprecedented. Moreover, the missionaries had expressly taught their converts that only passive resistance could ensure them a martyr's crown . . . other reasons were that the natural leaders of such a revolt, the Christian daimyō and higher samurai, were either dead or had recanted for the most part; whereas few of the peasants and farmers, who constituted the majority of the converts, possessed any weapons.[43]

Even the Shimabara Rebellion of 1637, which has often been cited as a Christian uprising, Boxer sees as a revolt caused by the "unbearable cruelty of the local daimyō's methods of tax collection."[44] And Asian specialist George Elison adds that this most manifest of Kirishitan revolutionary acts was, from the standpoint of the Christian teaching, quite heterodox and . . . the rebels, far from being guided by the Christian ideology were men who were desperate because they were spiritually rootless.

The eschatology of the Shimabara uprising was the common fantastic delusion of the poor, exploited and downtrodden. Their movement may be termed an eruption of social Chiliasm.[45]

Cousin's report, however, raises an important related point, namely, the different beliefs and practices of the Christian descendants. Neither Cousin nor any of the early French missionaries gets at the question of what happened during the years of hiding. How much Buddhism, Shintō, and Japanese folklore was interwoven with Christian beliefs and practices? Did a totally new religion develop as Christian teachings were passed from generation to generation? These are questions that the missionaries did not, perhaps could not, deal with.

Instead, in any number of instances, the priests accuse the kakure Kirishitan of culpable ignorance and obstinate refusal to correct their ways. One missionary says in 1893:

Those [kakure Kirishitan] that remain to be converted seem to be so obstinate in their blindness that it would take a miracle to open their eyes. . . . They still have the remembrance of their Christian origin, but outwardly they live like pagans, observing the Buddhist feasts, and conforming to the requirements of the Buddhist monasteries in which they are registered.[46]

The Japanese government comes under increasing attack and is seen as a hindrance in missionary work. Cousin, in 1893, complains of the government coldness and passivity toward the missionaries.[47]

It is not until 1894 that a more understanding and thoughtful view of the kakure Kirishitan situation is expressed in the French sources. In this year, one of the missionaries writes that the principal obstacle to the return of the kakure Kirishitan:

> at least in the countryside [where the majority lived] is the village organization. Each village, in effect, has leaders, who without holding an official title, can make the times good or bad at whim. There are rules to which the inhabitants must conform under pain of seeing themselves denied help in times of need, and robbed of all assistance in times of sickness. Those who would like to become Christian dare not for fear of arousing the ill will of their fellow citizens, and this fear, be it somewhat exaggerated, is not without foundation. It is necessary to convert these villages en bloc or at least [convert] a prominent part of the village.[48]

This is the first time one finds in the French sources a missionary coming to grips, in a sympathetic way, with Japanese civilization. The village structure the Japanese had lived in for centuries, is taken seriously and is seen as a valid concern in the individual's freedom to pursue a course of action that could lead to alienation.

This line of thinking is not pursued, however, and in 1900 we again find Sauret complaining about the Japanese and their government:

> The evangelization of Japan is not without difficulty. The national constitution authorizes, it is true, the preaching of Christianity. But the prejudice against foreign religions has disappeared only in language. The members of Japan's upper classes are generally too proud. As for the working class, one can only reach them with the help of catechists, Christians who are instructed and reliable

Japanese wearing the costume of the country, speaking the same language and working the same job as their compatriots.[49]

During the Russo-Japanese War (1904–05), the missionaries report that they and Japanese who were friendly to them are under attentive but discreet surveillance.[50] In 1906, the missionaries record instances of Christians being accused of a lack of patriotism because they refused to contribute to the decorations for the celebration of the anniversary of Jimmu Tennō, Japan's legendary first emperor.[51]

Then, in 1910–11, the high treason affair erupted (*taigyaku jiken*); the socialist Kōtoku Shūsui and eleven others were executed for allegedly plotting to assassinate Emperor Meiji. The missionaries explain the situation in the following way:

> An anarchist plot has thrown the authorities into a virtual panic. In each department [district], two police officers watch over the press and public meetings with the mission of preventing and repressing the blossoming of "dangerous ideas." Teachers have received the order to instill in youth the cult of the ancestors and of the heroes of the country; each day, processions of school children go to the Shintō temples [*sic*] guided by their teachers. We are witnessing a reaction of chauvinism that one would have thought dead.[52]

The missionaries' problems with the government were undoubtedly valid. During the 1890s Japan was becoming more sophisticated about things Western, and Japanese began exerting an independence of thought and action. Protestant converts of the time, most of them former samurai, were becoming increasingly restless under Western tutelage and showing a strong desire to achieve a self-image of equality with the West.[53] Their attitudes reflect the general feelings of the Japanese government. With the promulgation of the new constitution in 1889, there was a renewed sense of pride in the country, which grew with the Japanese success in the Sino-Japanese War (1894–95), the Anglo-Japanese Alliance (1902), and the Japanese victory in the Russo-Japanese War (1904–05). It is clear that the Japanese were coming to realize not only that Christianity was not necessary to Japanese success but that the period of Western superiority was drawing to a close.

The Japanese government's attitude toward Christianity cannot be held accountable, however, for the missionaries' failure among the kakure Kirishitan. Nor is it sufficient to say that fear, concern about reputation, self-interest, or lack of courage prevented the return of the kakure Kirishitan. The compact village structure certainly militated against individuals choosing to return to Catholicism if the majority of the villagers were kakure Kirishitan. But even this does not constitute an adequate explanation of the fact that thirty thousand Christian descendants chose to continue their religious practice as they had learned it from their ancestors.

It would seem that a more satisfying explanation for the failures of the French missionaries can be found, first by examining the degree of continuity between the religious life of the early Christians and that of the nineteenth-century kakure Kirishitan and second by viewing the kakure Kirishitan within the context of the traditional Japanese approach to religious belief.

Chapter
VI

# Understanding the Kakure Kirishitan

# Introduction

The preceding chapter underlines the fact that the French missionaries were unable to understand the position taken by the kakure Kirishitan. The "returned" Japanese Catholics were no more perceptive, seeing them as cut-off or separated from the true faith. The kakure Kirishitan were looked upon by both groups as souls close to salvation but destined for the fires of hell unless they acknowledged their errors and accepted the teachings of the Catholic church. In general, they were an enigma to believing Catholics.

We are now in position, however, to assess the kakure Kirishitan religion in a more objective manner first by comparing it to both the religion of their Christian ancestors and to the religious life demanded by the French missionaries, and then by looking at the kakure Kirishitan in the light of the traditional Japanese approach to religious belief.

# The Kakure Kirishitan and Christianity

One cannot help but be struck by the degree of continuity that existed between the religious life of the kakure Kirishitan and Japan's early Christians. The kakure Kirishitan maintained almost all of the practices stressed by the missionaries of the sixteenth and seventeenth centuries. They continued to rely on unordained men to perform services denied them in the absence of the priests—an absence that was the rule rather than the exception for early Christians. They therefore continued to administer baptism, to assist the dying in praying for salvation, to conduct funeral ceremonies, and to meet in homes to pray together. Each year they determined the important feastdays, many of which were clearly related to Christian feasts.

Among the prayers they recited, almost all can be traced to prayers of the Catholic church. On Ikitsuki, the members of the compania met monthly, in some places weekly, for a religious ceremony directly related to the recitation of the rosary, a practice encouraged by the priests as they formed the various confraternities.

The kakure Kirishitan also continued to see religious articles as important in their practice. In Ikitsuki and Hirado, these were the nandogami, while in the Gotōs and Kurosaki statues of the Kannon Bosatsu (the Buddhist "Goddess of Mercy") were discovered, statues the

Christians in hiding looked to as representations of the Virgin Mary.

There is continuity in the fact that these kakure Kirishitan did not consider themselves Buddhists or Shintoists but Kirishitan. They lived for the most part the way the missionaries taught their ancestors to live as the persecutions mounted. Considering that the persecutions began in earnest as early as 1597, one can conclude that many of those who went underground had lived most of their Christian life hiding and camouflaging their religious practice. Secrecy became a part of being Christian. Those Japanese who were converted in the earliest years of the mission when there was little reason for fear would have been very old or dead by 1639. Those elements of the Christian life that are lacking in the kakure Kirishitan practice are precisely those things that time and circumstances made impossible for the missionaries to stress—the sacraments, church law, and the notion of an institutional church.

Where the early missionaries had bent over backwards to adapt their proselytizing to Japanese culture, the nineteenth-century French missionaries demanded that the kakure Kirishitan reject not only the religious teachings of their ancestors but many of their cultural traditions as well.

Historical circumstances further complicated the work of the French missionaries. The church stand on the Rites Controversy forbade the priests to allow the Kirishitan to keep their *butsudan* (Buddhist household altar) and *kamidana* (Shintō household altar) despite the fact that many of these housed Christian artifacts. It also forbade compromise with existing Japanese beliefs and practices, though the times, especially the 1890s, made it more profitable for the missionaries to be and act Western than to try to adapt to the traditional Japanese mores. Yet the kakure Kirishitan, because they were poor, uneducated, and living in relatively secluded areas, remained tightly bound to Japanese tradition. They were not of the segment of the

Japanese population that clamored after Western knowledge and technology; and even if they had been, the missionaries would not have fared much better since they represented a church that rejected modern civilization.

Hence the nineteenth-century Catholic missionaries were in the paradoxical position of alienating those Japanese who wanted to learn the ways of the "modern" West and in turn alienating those Japanese whose cultural ties ran so deep that only one with a deep understanding of and sympathy for their traditions could reach them on any level, be it religious, political, or economic.

Because the French missionaries had virtually no motivation to achieve an understanding of traditional Japanese culture in general and of the kakure Kirishitan culture in particular, they failed to reach the majority of those kakure Kirishitan who initially rejected them. Their authoritarian stance on orthodox practice and on immediate repair of doubtful baptisms and faulty marriages and their insistence on the cessation of "pagan" rites was asking too much. They demanded much more, more quickly, of their converts than was ever the case in the first Christian period.

By 1890, there were 168 churches and chapels in Japan, and a ratio of 1 priest for every 450 Christians.[1] Access to priests and all aspects of Christian life (sacraments, liturgical worship, instruction) was more readily available than it was at any time during the sixteenth and seventeenth centuries. With no fear of further persecution after 1873, the missionaries could and did keep a watchful eye on the religious life of the Christians, and they insisted on correct and consistent practice of religious duties. The early missionaries had neither the time nor the numbers to be so watchful; their efforts to understand and adapt themselves and their teachings to Japanese culture weakened any tendency toward authoritarianism.

The Christianity lived underground and continued after the Tokugawa period by the kakure Kirishitan, then, was more closely aligned with the practice of Christianity during Japan's first Christian period than was the practice demanded by the French missionaries after 1865.

Despite the remarkable continuity of form or practice, the kakure Kirishitan possessed but a minimal understanding of Christian doctrine. As we have seen, some of the central notions of Christianity were lacking or misunderstood, such as the Trinity, one all-powerful creator-God, and the significance of the death and resurrection of Jesus Christ. The kakure Kirishitan did not understand the majority of the prayers they recited, and all festivals of Christian origin were commemorated without any cognizance of their original meaning. In the *Tenchi hajimari no koto*, the basic framework of the Christian story can be recognized by anyone possessing a certain degree of familiarity with it; yet, essential doctrinal elements are lacking or misinterpreted.

These misunderstandings can be explained by the fact that the early Christians, as we have argued, did not have sufficient time or freedom to come to a deep understanding of Christian teachings. But related to this explanation, the kakure Kirishitan seem to serve as an example of the general theory of cultural change that holds that "the form of a new culture element is more readily accepted than its associated meaning because form is more easily observed and imitated than meaning."[2] This is not to imply that the kakure Kirishitan accepted a form that was meaningless to them. Rather, the form presented by the missionaries did have meaning for them, but it was not necessarily the meaning intended or believed by the missionaries, as we will see below.

# The Kakure Kirishitan and Japanese Religion

The very elements of kakure Kirishitan practice that showed striking continuity with the early Christian period were the elements that could easily be identified with similar practices in Japanese culture: the religious hierarchy, the importance of baptism and the baptismal waters, the funeral services, the recitation of prayers, the rosary, the festivals, and the religious confraternities. These facts bear out a second theory of cultural change, namely, that "new cultural traits are accepted primarily on the basis of their utility and their compatibility with the existing cultural configuration."[3] The fact that those elements that the kakure Kirishitan found to be both useful in and compatible with their day-to-day life were the same elements stressed by the early missionaries underlines the degree to which the priests in the sixteenth and seventeenth centuries attempted to adapt Catholicism during the elementary stages of their proselytizing.

If we look at the more general characteristics of Japanese religion, however, we can better understand why the kakure Kirishitan chose to continue their own religion rather than accept the teachings of the nineteenth-century French missionaries. One must bear in mind that for most Japanese, the various religious traditions of Japan are not mutually exclusive.

Shintō has been seen as indigenous to Japan, although there are those who argue otherwise, and its emphasis on ritual cleanliness, respect for nature, and respect for ancestors have been extremely influential throughout Japanese history. With the introduction of Buddhism into Japan via Korea around A.D. 500, one might have expected a major religious clash. But the Japanese were able to reconcile the two beliefs, seeing Shintō *kami* (sacred spirits or divinities) as manifestations of the Buddha. So thoroughly did the two religious beliefs meld at the popular level that, Blacker argues, there is a large area of religious practice "in which the worshipper is scarcely aware whether the deity he is a addressing is Shintō *kami* or a bodhisattva." And she feels that this aspect of Japanese religion "has been either ignored or relegated to various snail patches with pejorative labels such as superstition, syncretism or magic."[4]

Within Buddhism itself, the Japanese have adapted the religion to such a degree that it is distinctively different from the Buddhism practiced in China and India and is therefore worthy of study in its own right. The same holds true for Confucianism, never popular as a religious belief in Japan but rather as a code of ethics the Japanese have adapted through the years to fit their changing government and social structures. The Taoist religion, likewise, never became a separate religion in Japan but was incorporated into many of the festivals and rituals on the folk level.

It is understandable, given this tradition, that the kakure Kirishitan would have found it natural to incorporate aspects of their Shintō, Buddhist, and folk past into the practice of Christianity. One might argue that the kakure Kirishitan were exclusive, forbidding marriage outside the religion and allowing only kakure Kirishitan into their religious observances. But this exclusivity was one aspect of their religious practice that came from Christianity, and it was reinforced during the Tokugawa period, in which secrecy was imperative for survival. By the nineteenth century, secrecy and exclusivity had become a part of kakure Kirishitan religion as it was taught by their ancestors. Hence, the kakure Kirishitan did what Japanese had been doing for centuries, incorporating elements from an already rich tradition into their Christianity or vice versa. Their exclusivity barred outsiders, but it did not bar their religious heritage.

Byron Earhart, a specialist on Japanese religion, has found at least six other characteristics in the traditional Japanese approach to religion, and in each case religion as it was practiced by the kakure Kirishitan remained within the tradition. First, he sees the harmony between the human race, the gods, and nature as a "cornerstone of religion."[5] The nandogami of the Ikitsuki Kirishitan were simple, everyday objects—hanging scrolls, San Juan water, the ofuda, the otempensia, paper crosses. The Christian saints, martyrs, and their own ancestors were all worshipped as gods. But the idea of a god set off, apart and above them, did not seem to be part of their belief structure. The importance of nature was evidenced in the number of festivals concerned with planting, harvesting, the wind, the rain, and insects.

Second, Japanese religion has stressed the importance of the family and family members, both living and dead.[6] We see this exemplified in the stress that the kakure Kirishitan placed on proper burial ceremonies, the importance attached to the observance of the death anniversaries, and the fact that they refused to rid their homes of the kamidana and the butsudan. Living members were drawn together through religious meetings and festival celebrations.

Third, throughout Japanese religious history, great significance has been attached to purification, rituals, and charms.[7] We have seen that each of these was important to the kakure Kirishitan practice. The kakure Kirishitan purified homes and fields, they recited a set of prayers at the various religious festivals, and their omaburi, ofuda, and otempensia were used much as charms had been used in traditional Japan: to cure illness, to protect fields and harvests, and to drive out evil spirits.

A fourth characteristic of Japanese religion is the prevalence of festivals and the pride taken in local cults or celebrations.[8] We have seen the importance of festival celebrations among the kakure Kirishitan, and we have seen festivals celebrated in one area that contained elements not found in another area. For example, there was the "San Juan no uta" (St. John's Song), unique to Yamada, the reverence for Basutean in Kurosaki, and the place of honor afforded Jizō-korai in the Gotō Islands.

The fifth common element cited by Earhart, the weaving of religion into everyday life, is exemplified in the above four points.[9] It has never been a tradition in Japanese religion to demand weekly attendance at a temple or shrine. Rather the believer worshipped in the home or the field, and made formal visits to the local temple or shrine only at certain times—after the birth of a child, for funeral or memorial services, to seek some special favor or blessing. For the kakure Kirishitan of Ikitsuki, the regular meeting of the compania reflected both the teaching of the missionaries and the voluntary religious associations (kō) dating from medieval Japan.

Finally, Earhart says that there was a "natural bond between Japanese religion and the Japanese nation."[10] The kakure Kirishitan, living in relatively remote areas, did not seem to exemplify so much a consciousness of the Japanese nation as they exemplified the desire to maintain their Japanese traditions. The importance of their ancestors and the duty to carry on the teachings of their ancestors appeared to be uppermost in their minds. But because the notion of Japanese nation was tied so closely to a respect for Japan's ancestral tradition, beginning with the emperor, one might argue that this last characteristic of Japanese religion was exemplified, at least indirectly, by the kakure Kirishitan.

Thus, the kakure Kirishitan came into the nineteenth century practicing their religion as they had learned it from their Christian ancestors and much the same as it had been practiced during the first Christian period. At the same time, they had melded it into the traditional Japanese approach to religious life. They were not willing to let go of the Christian elements, nor were they willing to give up their Japanese traditions. What they had done, in essence, was to make their Christian religion Japanese.

The Catholic church that the nineteenth-century kakure Kirishitan encountered was not the church of the missionaries who converted their ancestors. The Rites Controversy had destroyed whatever hope had existed for adapting Catholicism to a culture other than Western European. The Catholic church would not accommodate the kakure Kirishitan, nor would the kakure Kirishitan accommodate the Catholic church. Their respective paths had grown too far apart. While the kakure Kirishitan grew within the teachings of their ancestors and within the traditions of Japan, the church broke away from the promising style of men like Francis Xavier, Alexandro Valignano, and Matteo Ricci. The kakure Kirishitan found their path fulfilling and satisfying and ignored the church. The church meanwhile, unable and unwilling to ignore the kakure Kirishitan, found only frustration.

Chapter
VII

# The Kakure Kirishitan Compared to Other Japanese Christian Groups

# Introduction

How do the kakure Kirishitan compare with other Christian-rooted groups in Japan during our time frame? Three works that discuss Japanese Christianity will serve as comparative studies to help answer this question. Each group studied, despite showing marked contrasts with the kakure Kirishitan, is similar enough to provide for a fruitful comparison. Also, this discussion is limited to broad comparative strokes rather than detail. The value of comparison is to open new avenues for discussion.[1]

# Protestant Christian Groups

The first study concentrates on three Protestant groups. In contrast to the Catholic church, which in essence rejected the modern world of the nineteenth century, the various Protestant denominations embraced the scientific and industrial revolution. The early Protestant missionaries who came to Japan were often highly educated and accomplished people. Their early converts came primarily from the former samurai class[2] and young people studying English in the mission schools. As a result, Protestant converts were more highly placed and influential than Catholic converts. Yet it is clear that neither Protestants nor Catholics were overwhelmingly successful in the conversion process. Why is this, given the immense amounts of money and personnel poured into Japan during the Meiji Era? In the Protestant endeavor, which more clearly carried the message of the newly modernizing world along with its Christianity, what prevented more Japanese from embracing Christianity?

This question is asked by social scientist Kiyomori Morioka[3] in a study he conducted of three rural churches: the Annaka Church, a Congregational church founded in 1878 in western Gumma Prefecture; the Shimamura Church, an American Methodist Episcopal church founded in 1887 in Gumma Prefecture; and Kusakabe Church, a Canadian Methodist church founded in 1896 in

Yamanashi Prefecture. In each case, Morioka asks three questions: "What was the social and individual character of those who embraced Christianity? Second, what was the source and the nature of the pressure on Christian converts? Third, were there elements intimately related with 'modal behavior' in the activities of the Christians?"[4] (He posits that Christianity is still seen as "deviant behavior" even today whereas Buddhism became "modal behavior" over the years.) Although Morioka does not define his terms in the article, it is assumed here that by "modal" he means "occurring most frequently in a sample population" and by "deviant" he means "diverging from the normal social and religious standards of behavior."

Morioka's findings are briefly as follows. In the case of the Annaka Church, the majority of the converts were former samurai. For example, in the first forty-four converts, only five were not samurai. Among the five was the administrative head of a neighboring village, also a manufacturer of bean paste and soy sauce in town, and his wife; this man was ahead of his time in many ways, so in that sense Morioka sees him as "deviant" even before conversion. Between 1878 and 1887 among the 446 persons baptized, few were peasants or laborers. "It was only among those classes interested in new ideas, impressed by the highly ethical lives led by Christians, and preoccupied with imitating this ethic themselves who were attracted to Christianity."[5]

The Shimamura church was in a center of the silkworm-egg industry. Between 1886 and 1900 there were 111 converts: owners of silkworm-egg industries, their families, servants and branch households, and other converts. In the second group it was usual for the entire household to convert if the head did. With the decline of the silkworm-egg industry came the decline of the church. Clearly, "the attendant advantages of a broader outlook and increasing wealth [which came with

Christianity] was undeniably one of the factors conducive to this deviant behavior [conversion to Christianity]."[6]

Finally, the last church in Morioka's study, the one at Kusakabe, experienced 145 baptisms between 1896 and 1907. The church membership is typified by three of its early members, all industrial and commercial leaders in industries that were not limited by the local community, such as sericulture, silkworm-egg industry, and silk-reeling manufacture.

Morioka comes to two conclusions from these studies. Briefly, it was the people of the literate upper and middle class that converted, people who, possibly because of their occupations, had a more urban orientation. Second, it was the individual attitude of these converts and not their class that proved decisive in their conversion. The majority of this class did not convert, so the converts were seen as "deviant." This being the case, what pressures did these converts suffer in the village because of their religious practice?

To answer, Morioka first explains the importance of the religion of the household (*hito-gami*) and the religion of the local community (*uji-gami*). The former consisted of Buddhist rituals for the dead, and the latter, the many festivals centered around Shintō worship involving prayers for planting, harvest, and prosperity in general. To engage in these rituals and festivals represented the norm in terms of village behavior. But having embraced Christianity, the convert was expected to relinquish these practices, putting one in a difficult position in the village. For example, the neighbors were offended when converts burned their household altars or, worse yet, hid them in a corner of the outhouse; to disassociate from the local Shintō shrine was tantamount to removing oneself from village social life.[7] The villagers therefore pressured these Christians in a variety of ways.

The pressures Christians suffered in the three churches came primarily from three areas. First, the head of the household had enormous influence over members: if he did not convert, neither could individuals for the most part. Second, the community taunted or ostracized the Christians. Third, persecution came from Buddhists through anti-Christian lectures and determination of grave sites. This latter point centered on the fact that before becoming Christian, these upper- or middle-class people had plots at the Buddhist temple; but the Buddhist priests either refused them burial in the temple or insisted they be buried by a Buddhist priest if they wanted to use their plot.[8]

How then did these Christians manage in their society? Morioka points out areas where they did practice "modal behavior" intertwined with their "deviant behavior" and areas where their "deviant behavior" became "modal behavior." He gives examples of the former. In Kusakabe, many Christians continued making presents to the priests at the Bon Festival and at the year's end. Also, some had both Buddhist and Christian rites at burial. In Shimamura and Kusakabe, Christians shared in the expenses of the Shintō shrine to help support festivals for the community deities, even though they did not visit the shrine on those days. Some Christians, especially as the churches aged, retained their Shintō and Buddhist household altars, treating them respectfully and using them again as their Christian faith weakened. In Annaka and Shimamura, Christians contracted with the Buddhist temple to pay for the use of their burial spots. Finally, it appears that a good number of Christians continued folk religious practices and held memorial services according to Buddhist tradition, for the Bon Festival and the equinoxes. Morioka does not indicate if these accommodations were acceptable to the church hierarchy, but one would be inclined to think not.

By "deviant behavior" becoming "modal" Morioka means practices or institutions that originated with the Christian churches that were taken over by the Buddhists or by other non-Christians. Examples are a Christian reform movement that focused on abstinence from alcohol and tobacco, and the observance of monogamy in both the Annaka church and the Shimamura church; an antiprostitution campaign in the Annaka church, which in 1893 succeeded in crushing the opposition (a member of the Shimamura church also helped in this crusade); institutions such as a girls' high school and Sunday schools. Once out of the hands of Christians, these schools became acceptable to the village.

In response to the first question he raised, namely why were there not more conversions, he concludes that "Christians' deviant behavior, which has been subjected to social pressure, lost prominence as it was syncretized, whereas their deviant behavior provoking social respect or envy became widely accepted and absorbed into modal behavior. Through these processes, the unique characteristics of Christianity in the early Meiji period were eventually lost."[9] In discussing why more lower-class Japanese did not convert, Morioka suggest two reasons. First, the church was seen as a rather exclusive club, and lower-class villagers felt neither comfortable nor welcome. Second, the upper-class villagers were better able to handle the pressures caused by their "deviant behavior."[10]

How do these findings relate to the kakure Kirishitan? Two important factors here are locale and time. In terms of locality, the kakure Kirishitan living in rural areas would be in somewhat the same position as these Christian communities. However, in terms of deviant and modal behavior, it is important to remember that their ancestors during the Tokugawa period had to adopt modal behavior for survival and their deviant behavior was completely hidden. Put another way, they had to give every indication to non-Christians that they also were non-Christians, which meant full use of their household altars, and full participation in village festivals related to Buddhist, Shintō, and folk traditions. What happened over the years was that these Kirishitan passed along a religious tradition in which their deviant behavior of hiding religious practices became modal for them. It was part of the practice, so that when the ban against Christianity was lifted in 1873, they continued to practice their religion in secret while participating fully in the Buddhist, Shintō, and folk traditions of their villages.

There is an obvious difference in terms of time. The kakure Kirishitan passed their religious tradition along over seven generations, while the churches studied here did not begin their existence until the last quarter of the nineteenth century. It is interesting that in Morioka's study there is a move to reinstate the household altars and to continue participation in the local festivals within the first two generations simply due to village pressure. This shows, it would seem, the tremendous power exerted by the village. Perhaps Morioka's Christians did not have to accommodate to save their physical lives, as did the kakure Kirishitan, but did so rather to save their social life in the village. By the time of the Meiji era, the source of pressure on the kakure Kirishitan was coming not from the village but from the French missionaries, who viewed them as "separated" and "worse than the pagans."

Even though the French missionaries could recognize clear Christian influences in their practice and prayers, the kakure Kirishitan understanding of the religion was different enough to cause the French priests to demand a return to orthodox practice. The kakure Kirishitan refused, believing that what was asked was no less than a rejection of the religious life of their ancestors. As in the Christian groups studied by Morioka, we see in the kakure Kirishitan groups the same influence exerted by the head of the household vis-à-vis the French missionaries. If the head of the household did not return to orthodox practice, neither did his household. However, unlike Morioka's subjects, the kakure Kirishitan in the Meiji period were not former samurai or upper- or middle-class people but rather were poor farmers and fisherfolk. They would have had no incentive to abandon a religious practice that apparently was meaningful to them. They were not the up-and-coming leaders of the new Japan. And even if they had been, the religion of choice for social climbing in Meiji Japan was not Roman Catholicism.

Within their villages, the kakure Kirishitan were assimilated and accepted as part of the community during the Tokugawa period. As it came to light, however, that these people were continuing the secret practice of their religion, they were seen as deviant by the returned Christians, first because they called themselves Kirishitan and second because of the strange form of Christianity they were practicing. Their continued practice in secret caused mainstream Japanese to see them as deviant. But then, living in small villages near Nagasaki and on the offshore islands of Kyūshū, it was not their practice alone that set them apart from mainstream Japan.

# Mukyōkaı (ṇon-Church Movement)

A second study that attempts a framework for analyzing a Christian religion in Japan is that used by Carlo Caldarola, also a social scientist, in his study of the Mukyōkai, the Non-Church Movement of Uchimura Kanzō (1861–1930).[11] In this work Caldarola uses the theoretical framework of acculturation, which he defines as "a complex process of interaction between two cultures the nature of which does not depend solely on the intersecting elements. Equally important are the type and context of the interactions, the selective processes which develop on either side, and the eventual results of the process."[12] Caldarola suggests four possible results of the acculturation process. First, alienation, where one rejects the traditional culture but does not fully accept the new and thus remains marginal to both cultures; as an example, he cites the Native Americans. Second is reorientation, which involves more movement toward the new culture and necessitates rejecting elements of the old even while remaining in the old cultural context. Third, reaffirmation "sees members of a society attempting to revive or perpetuate elements of the indigenous tradition by reinforcing them with elements borrowed from the alien culture."[13] The fourth is integration, a process that may evolve "new cultural traits—elements which did not exist in either culture prior to their interaction."[14]

During the Meiji period, Uchimura's stance resulted in both alienation and reorientation, since in founding the Mukyōkai, he rejected the structure of the Christian church, including priests, sacraments, and churches, but held on to the Bible and fellowship with Jesus Christ. He thus alienated himself and his followers from the Western Christian church. In turn, he alienated himself from Japanese culture, first by an act of *lèse majesté* in refusing to bow before a portrait of the emperor at the First Higher School in Tokyo where he was teaching (1891) and then by becoming an antiwar spokesman at the time of the Russo-Japanese War.[15] Previous to these acts, he went through reaffirmation after spending time in the United States, where some of his illusions about Christianity were shattered. In America, which called itself a Christian country, he encountered much that did not meet his ideal of Christianity. "Do but make the Chinese and Japanese keep the commandments of their own Confucius, and you make fairer Christendoms of these two nations than any you have in Europe or America. The best of Christian converts has never given up the essence of Buddhism or Confucianism. We welcome Christianity because it helps us to become more like our own ideals."[16]

The Mukyōkai eventually reached the stage of integration. A major part of that integration resulted because, for Uchimura, to be Japanese was of great importance, but he had to be Japanese without compromising the high ideals he had found in Christianity. Simply stated, he felt he had to do what Jesus commanded him to do as set down in the Sermon on the Mount. To this he added the concept of Bushidō—a combination that he saw as "'the finest product in the world.'"[17] Today, Caldarola says that Japanese see the Mukyōkai as "truly Japanese."[18]

The kakure Kirishitan can be compared to the Mukyōkai members in their move toward a religion that has no priests, no sacraments except for baptism, and no churches. Their religion had formed itself over the years to the point where it was not accepted or acknowledged as Christian by the Roman Catholic church, and some of the practices and religious objects they retained differed from those of any other Japanese religious groups. Originally, like the Mukyōkai, they moved through reorientation, where they had to reject elements of the old; but once they were underground, Tokugawa law forced upon them the process of reaffirmation, where they perpetuated Buddhist and Shintō elements and secretly added Christian practices. Over the years, what they have come to is an amalgam of Christianity and Japanese religions.

The kakure Kirishitan differ from the Mukyōkai in that the integration they reached was not a conscious choice, as Uchimura's was, but rather due to a twist of history that put them in most unusual circumstances. Their ancestors quite consciously engaged in a camouflage process as a defense against authorities (e.g., the Kannon Bosatsu became Maria Kannon; two burial ceremonies, one Christian and one Buddhist; and so on). By Meiji times, the camouflage had been passed along as traditional practice. Originally there was only the struggle to survive persecution. Through the years, we encounter the same type of integration of Christian and Japanese elements that was consciously carried out by Uchimura. In Caldarola's schema, one would have to argue that the kakure Kirishitan practice, like that of the Mukyōkai, has become completely Japanese.

An interesting development in the Mukyōkai is the split that occurred after World War II, a split that speaks to the nature of Japanese religious belief and practice, and more directly, perhaps, to the Kirishitan situation than the Mukyōkai. Called the Makuya (Tabernacle of Christ), it retains the Mukyōkai rejection of priests, sacraments, and churches and retains the emphasis on the Bible study groups. It differs in that its membership is primarily those who are less educated than Mukyōkai members and who come from a lower social class. It was founded by Teshima Ikurō (1910–1973), who through a series of life experiences felt called to lead a new form of Mukyōkai, one less cold and abstract, more in touch with experience. His movement emphasizes "the presence of the Holy Spirit through healing and speaking in tongues," grafting "a pentecostal form of Christianity on to the popular tradition of Japan."[19]

The Makuya movement is appropriate to our discussion here because in less than sixty years the Mukyōkai already has a splinter group that reaches a more popular, experiential level. Its move was not back to an institutional Christian church but rather toward an empowerment of the people, a drawing in of those of lower social status. The movement continues the disassociation with Western Christianity. It is doing what the kakure Kirishitan did somewhat by nature over the years of hiding, bringing theory to the level of practice for believers, while theory and abstraction become less and less important.

# Orthodoxy and heterodoxy

A third study is that of Takeda Kiyoko, an intellectual historian, who sees Uchimura's church as an "indigenous Japanese type of 'sect' movement."[20] Takeda uses "indigenous" in the sense of the Christian gospel becoming "rooted in the spiritual soil of the Japanese people, as though it had been raised there."[21] Today, she goes on to say, the Japanese generally regard the Mukyōkai as among the orthodox Christian groups; she makes no mention of the Makuya movement. Takeda's frame of reference is the notion of orthodoxy and heterodoxy, and she attempts to discuss a type of Japanese Christianity that she sees as being between orthodoxy and heterodoxy. Underlying the relativity of such terms she reminds us of Bp. William Warburton saying to Lord Sandwich in Priestly's *Memoirs*: "Orthodoxy, my Lord . . . is my doxy—heterodoxy is another man's doxy."[22] Christian orthodoxy in Takeda's argument "is the position of those who claim to profess a faith and doctrine consistent with the scriptures thereby embracing the truth of God's salvation."[23] Heterodoxy is obviously, viewed from the orthodox point of view, any deviation from that faith and doctrine.

Those who stand between orthodoxy and heterodoxy, according to Takeda, are "those who find themselves dissatisfied with Christian orthodoxy in Japan, or for some other reason stumble in their faith and therefore decide to abandon Christian belief."[24] They do not proclaim a new orthodoxy, as Uchimura Kanzō did. Rather, they seemingly abandon totally their Christian life and plunge themselves into Japan's secular culture. They are not "completely apathetic or actively hostile to Christianity."[25] Takeda sees these people as free to forge new ground between orthodoxy and heterodoxy while retaining values derived from Christianity. They are uniquely suited to providing insights "into methods and approaches through which the traditional Japanese ethos might be penetrated and reformed from within, and a truly effective dialogue initiated between the indigenous ethos of Japan and Christianity."[26] (This latter point is the reason for her essay.)

To reach this state, there must be apostasy, and Takeda has several categories of apostasy. The people she sees between orthodoxy and heterodoxy fall into an apostasy that Takeda calls "disillusioned apostasy" or into another group who, unnamed, reject Christian orthodoxy but never really pretended to embrace it; one might call them "fellow travelers." In the first group she puts such people as the novelist Arishima Takeo (1878–1923), who "found that he could not tolerate a Christian church that was suffused with non-Christian elements, and came to doubt his own belief, so he moved off into humanism and a quest for modern selfhood."[27] Also in this group is the activist Miyazaki Tōten (1871–1922), who "could not be satisfied with the traditional Christian view of society and its solutions to social problems, and threw himself into the struggle for revolution in Asia as a comrade of Sun Yat-sen."[28] In the second group, Takeda mentions Sōma Kokkō, the proprietor of the Nakamuraya Bakery in Shinjuku, who "gravitated toward reliance on salvation by Amida in her effort to develop a new commercial ethic."[29]

The kakure Kirishitan, Takeda says, fall into the category of "disguised apostasy,"[30] because they never internally renounced their Catholic faith, even though outwardly they professed Buddhism. She does not discuss the group that refused the teachings of the nineteenth-century missionaries nor their on-going life as kakure Kirishitan. Had she included them, one suspects she would have placed them with Uchimura Kanzō's Muk-yōkai, namely an indigenous type of Japanese "sect." By rejecting the teachings of the French missionaries, they had no connection with the Roman Catholic church and have none today, while their practices combine clearly discernible elements of both Christian and Japanese religious practices. They have not "left" the Catholic church, yet they are no longer a part of it. Can one be an apostate without taking a stand? Perhaps Takeda would argue that their stand as apostates was the rejection of the advances of the French missionaries. These Kirishitan, however, believed that what was handed down to them through their ancestors was the true faith. Therefore, it seems preferable not to call them apostates, nor should one call them heretics.

# Finding a Place for the Kakure Kirishitan

What then shall we call them? Using the studies of the three authors discussed above, we have tried to fit the kakure Kirishitan into each author's schema. That process, along with the comparison of the kakure Kirishitan to several Christian groups, highlights the following points. Like the Christians in Morioka's study, the kakure Kirishitan have combined their Christian religious practices with traditional Japanese practices. Like Uchimura Kanzō's Mukyōkai, their religion is devoid of priests, sacraments (with the exception of baptism), and churches. In developing a truly Japanese religion, they, like the Mukyōkai and the Makuya, have broken away from Western churches. Even the Christian elements that are recognizable are equally recognizable as coming from Japanese tradition, necessary because the kakure Kirishitan had to hide their practice. And it is their religious practice that has remained important, not an ideological stance. This practice combines elements of Buddhist, Shintō, Christian, and folk practice. Since they needed their Buddhist and Shintō altars in the home for camouflage, these remained in Meiji times despite the insistence of the French missionaries that they be removed. Each of these elements works toward defining them as a Japanese folk religion. Given these facts, one sees no other option but to call them an indigenous type of Japanese folk religion.

At the same time, they are unique. They never attempted to develop a new religion. They never decided to create their own priests to replace the missionaries or the few native clergy that were ordained before the closure of the country. It seems they attempted to live out their Catholic faith as they had been taught, yet what evolved was something new. And they continue to this day to practice in secret even though people generally know who and where they are. The secrecy of their practices is as much a part of the religion as the actual practices. Finally, they are dying out. In all probability, they will not survive long into the twenty-first century, if indeed they endure that long. They are an example of a largely unconscious blending of Christianity with traditional Japanese folk religion creating a new entity that by its very nature, village-bound and secret, prevents its continuance.

In some ways, the kakure Kirishitan seem to be part of a drama being acted out. The directors—first the missionaries, then the Tokugawa authorities, then again the missionaries—each had a part in staging the play. But the actors, the kakure Kirishitan, ran away with the script. Perhaps one can argue that, actually, the kakure Kirishitan in Meiji times belonged to Takeda's category of those who fell between orthodoxy and heterodoxy. Although she is dealing with persons who took an intellectual stance that put them on new ground, free to create new configurations, could her schema be applied on the level of folk religion or to people who were forced to new ground and unconsciously evolved a new, unique entity? And might one not ask whether indeed a dialogue could have been initiated between the French missionaries and these kakure Kirishitan if the Catholic church had not been the rigidly orthodox church that it was in the nineteenth century? Clearly, we cannot answer that question, but we can lament a marvelous opportunity lost to history because the directors did not know what to do with the improvisation that had gone on offstage.

The curtain may be about to come down on the kakure Kirishitan drama. But the playbook clearly teaches us something of what religion is for the Japanese. It teaches us something about the strength of village life. It teaches us something about the resiliency and creativity of the Japanese people. It sheds some light on what it means to be Japanese. Equally clearly, it shows how the orthodox nature of Christianity made dialogue between Christianity and Japanese religions extremely difficult. Takeda's notion of finding some ground between orthodoxy and heterodoxy seems the most fertile area for discussion. But until the Western Christian churches can be more open to change, dialogue will continue to be difficult. The Meiji era was ripe for such discussion. Whether such an ideal moment will again present itself is questionable.

# Conclusion: A Personal Reflection

The kakure Kirishitan, an estimated fifteen thousand to twenty thousand people, continue to practice their religion today in remote areas of Kyūshū and on its offshore islands. After 1889, conversions to Catholicism virtually ceased. The kakure Kirishitan have not felt it necessary to become members of the Buddhist or Shintō religions,[1] finding their own religious life and beliefs sufficient.

However, the future of the kakure Kirishitan religion is not promising. In the Gotō Islands, a newspaper reporter writing in 1968 quotes a kakure Kirishitan, a chōkata, describing how the group meetings of the neighboring village had been discontinued within the last several years because the village chōkata had died and there was no one to succeed him.[2] I visited an eighty-five-year-old mizukata at his home in Higashikashiyama (Sotome) in the summer of 1975, and he told me that he had performed approximately sixty baptisms since assuming the position in 1953, but that he had performed no baptisms since 1965. Further, the mizukata has no one to succeed him.[3]

Ikitsuki continues to be the most populous and best organized of the kakure Kirishitan settlements, but certain changes in recent years may indicate a weakening of the religion. For example, because of the expense involved, the Dōyonakayori has been discontinued, and the festival dates decided at that time are now decided at the Kazadome Ganjōju no orei (a festival for protection against destructive winds). The Osejo matsuri, once one of the most important festivals in Ikitsuki, is no longer continued for a ten-day period but is confined to three or four days.

More critical, however, is the fact that the young people of Ikitsuki and, for that matter, most of the young people in the hidden Kirishitan villages are not terribly interested in carrying on the practices of their parents. In the spring of 1980, I visited a tsumoto household on Ikitsuki and spoke both to the former head of the tsumoto and his wife. The seventy-year-old ottosama was quite ill, and his wife explained that the position of heading the tsumoto was very demanding. She blamed her husband's illness on his former duties. She also indicated that those days were difficult for her too. Because of the taboos during certain festival times, she, as wife of the ottosama, was not allowed to change her children's diapers or do the wash. Therefore, help had to come in. The two of them talked about the difficult struggle they had convincing their son to assume his father's post. The difficulties of the post were underlined when I visited what looked like a storehouse. It was built as a tsumoto by the people of Ikitsuki because the ottosama in charge of the area had run away and they needed a place to house the nandogami.

Another kakure Kirishitan on the island, a much younger man, indicated that many of the kakure Kirishitan do not baptize their children now, because if the children leave the island, it is imperative, in the event of death, that services be held in Ikitsuki. He indicated that this was simply becoming too complicated. He himself has three sons and a daughter, and only the eldest son is baptized. He felt that the practices would die out in his generation.

Many young people in kakure Kirishitan villages are no longer willing to be outside the mainstream of "modern" Japanese life and are moving to Tokyo and other large cities. Because the kakure Kirishitan religious practice is still performed in secret and is so totally bound up in the group meetings and local festival celebrations, it is not practiced in cities. The fact that so many young people are leaving their villages makes marriage within the religion increasingly difficult. It is equally difficult to find young people willing to learn the prayers so that they will be prepared to succeed to the official posts. Japanese scholars who have spent time studying the kakure Kirishitan believe it is only a matter of time before the kakure Kirishitan religion dies out. The kakure Kirishitan who remain in their villages, however, continue to be committed to their religious beliefs.[4]

The Catholic church has also undergone changes since the nineteenth century. Reversing the stand taken in the Rites Controversy, the church, at the Second Vatican Council (1963–65), endorsed the need for the adaptation of Catholicism to the cultural life of a people.[5] Although the idea is couched in guarded words and the dangers are enumerated, it puts the church on a path that could lead to an understanding of Japan's kakure Kirishitan. But any hope of the kakure Kirishitan and the Catholic church becoming of one mind appears to have been lost in nineteenth-century Japan.

# Epilogue

When the great Rabbi Israel Baal Shem-Tov saw misfortune threatening the Jews it was his custom to go into a certain part of the forest to meditate. There he would light a fire, say a special prayer, and the miracle would be accomplished and the misfortune averted.

Later, when his disciple, the celebrated Magid of Mezritch, had occasion, for the same reason, to intercede with heaven, he would go to the same place in the forest and say: "Master of the Universe, listen! I do not know how to light the fire, but I am still able to say the prayer." And again the miracle would be accomplished.

Still later, Rabbi Moshe-Leib of Sasov, in order to save his people once more, would go into the forest and say: "I do not know how to light the fire, I do not know the prayer, but I know the place and this must be sufficient." It was sufficient and the miracle was accomplished.

Then it fell to Rabbi Israel of Rizhyn to overcome misfortune. Sitting in his armchair, his head in his hands, he spoke to God: "I am unable to light the fire and I do not know the prayer; I cannot even find the place in the forest. All I can do is to tell the story, and this must be sufficient." And it was sufficient.

God made man because he loves stories.

from *The Gates of the Forest*
by Elie Wiesel[1]

# notes

## Introduction

[1] Kōya Tagita, *Shōwa jidai no sempuku Kirishitan* [Hidden Christians in the Showa era] (Tokyo: Nihon Gakujutsu Shinkokai, 1954), 1, 2. Hereafter cited as SJSK.

[2] *Kakure Kirishitan rekishi to minzoku* [Hidden Christians: history and customs] (Tokyo: Nihon Hōsō Shuppan Kyōkai, 1967).

[3] *Kakure Kirishitan* (Tokyo: Shibundo, 1959).

[4] Cited in William Madson, *Christo-Paganism: A Study of Mexican Religious Syncretism*, reprinted from Publication 19, 105–80, Middle American Research Institute (New Orleans: Tulane University, 1957), 1.

[5] H. Byron Earhart, *Japanese Religion: Unity and Diversity*, The Religious Life of Man Series (Belmont, California: Dickenson Publishing Company, Inc., 1969), 5–8.

[6] During the early Christian period, only Catholic missionaries proselytized in Japan. Protestant sects did not begin work there until the latter half of the ninteenth century.

## Chapter 1

[1] Fernand Mourret, S.S., *A History of the Catholic Church*, vol. 5, trans. Newton Thompson (St. Louis: B. Herder Book Co., 1930), 543–44.

[2] Newman C. Eberhardt, C.M., *A Summary of Catholic History*, vol. 2 (St. Louis: B. Herder Book Co., 1962), 230.

[3] Philip Hughes, *A Popular History of the Catholic Church* (New York: Macmillan Company, 1949), 179.

[4] Hubert Cieslik, S.J., "Early Jesuit Missionaries in Japan (II): Balthasar Gago and Japanese Christian Terminology," *Missionary Bulletin* 8 (May–June 1954), 86.

[5] Ibid.

⁶ Ibid., 88. It is interesting to note here that Matteo Ricci's solution for this problem in China was to form new, rather strange combinations of Chinese characters to express Christian ideas.

⁷ George B. Sansom, *The Western World and Japan* (New York: Alfred A. Knopf, 1950), 222.

⁸ Jesús Lopez-Gay, S.J., *El catecumenado en la mision del Japon del XVI* (Rome: Pontifical Gregorian University, 1966), 15–16. (I was assisted in the reading of this work by Kateri O'Shea, Associate Professor of Spanish at Loyola University Chicago and Mary C. Stretch, Executive Director for Business Executives for Economic Justice, Chicago.) In 1579, it is estimated that there were approximately 130,000 Japanese Christians and 55 Jesuits, only 23 of them priests.

⁹ Ibid., 18–19.

¹⁰ Ibid., 20–21.

¹¹ Ibid., 13–14.

¹² George Elison, *Deus Destroyed: The Image of Christianity in Early Modern Japan* (Cambridge: Harvard University Press, 1973), 36.

¹³ Jesús Lopez-Gay, S.J., "The Pre-Evangelization in the First Years of the Japan Mission," *Missionary Bulletin* 18 (1964): 587.

¹⁴ Elison, 36.

¹⁵ Johannes Laures, S.J., comp., *Kirishitan Bunko: A Manual of Books and Documents on the Early Christian Mission in Japan*, Monumenta Nipponica Monographs no. 5, 3rd edition (Tokyo: Sophia University Press, 1957), 42.

¹⁶ C. R. Boxer, *The Christian Century in Japan, 1549–1650* (Berkeley: University of California Press, 1951), 190.

¹⁷ Lopez-Gay, *El catecumenado*, 42–44.

¹⁸ Ibid., 60.

¹⁹ For examples, see ibid., 98–103.

[20] Ibid., 67.

[21] Ibid., 70.

[22] Ibid., 71.

[23] Elison, 35.

[24] Ibid., 15.

[25] Ibid., 55–56. For more detail on Cabral and Alexandro Valignano see Josef Franz Schütte, S.J., *Valignano's Mission Principles for Japan*, 2 vols., trans. John J. Coyne, S.J. (St. Louis: The Institute of Sources, 1980).

[26] Ibid., 16.

[27] Ibid., 17.

[28] Elison, 56–64.

[29] Lopez-Gay, *El catecumenado*, 145–52.

[30] Ibid., 149.

[31] Ibid., 174–75.

[32] Cerqueira remained in Japan until 1614. The first bishop to arrive in Japan was Bp. Pedro Martins. He reached Japan in August 1596 and was forced to leave in March 1597. For details see Joseph Jennes, C.I.C.M., *A History of the Catholic Church in Japan from its Beginnings to the Early Meiji Era*, revised ed. (Tokyo: Oriens Institute for Religious Research, 1973), 65–66; 235–36.

[33] Lopez-Gay, *El catecumenado,* 183–84.

[34] Elison, 71.

[35] Jennes, 239.

[36] Ibid.

[37] These ratios are based on numbers of priests and converts given in Boxer, Elison, and Jennes.

[38] Jennes, 24–25.

[39] Jennes, 132. The Franciscans began work in Japan in 1593, and the Dominicans and Augustinians arrived in 1602.

40 Arimichi Ebisawa, "Crypto-Christianity in Tokugawa Japan," *Japan Quarterly* 7, no. 3 (July–September 1960), 291.

41 Lopez-Gay, *El catecumenado*, 220.

42 Cited in ibid.

43 Ibid., 222.

44 Ibid., 222–24.

45 Ibid., 217–18.

46 Ibid., 194.

47 Some Franciscan missionaries administered the sacrament of confirmation with the permission of Rome, but this caused unrest among Japanese Christians. See T. Uyttenbroeck, O.F.M., *Early Franciscans in Japan*, Missionary Bulletin Series, vol. 6 (Himeji, Japan: Committee of the Apostolate, 1958), 35–36.

48 Summary here based on a photocopy of the *Konchirisan* given to the author by Kataoka Yakichi, summer 1975. Text also available in *Kirishitan sho, hai-yo sho* [Kirishitan and anti-Christian writings], ed. Ebisawa Arimichi et al., *Nihon shisō taikei* 25 (Tokyo: Iwanami, 1970), 361–80.

49 Laures, 91.

50 For text of this ban, see Elison, 115–16.

51 For text of this edict, see Jennes, 116–18.

52 Boxer, 336.

53 For texts of these edicts see David John Lu, *Sources of Japanese History*, vol. 1 (New York: McGraw-Hill Book Company, 1974), 216–18, and Boxer, 439–40.

54 Jennes, 164–66.

55 Ibid., 166–67.

56 Ibid., 167.

57 Laures, 90.

58 Ibid., 241, 245.

59 Boxer, 339.

# Chapter 2

1 Tagita, SJSK, 7.

2 Naojiro Murakami, "An Old Church Calendar in Japanese," *Monumenta Nipponica* 5, no. 1 (1942): 220–21.

3 Some believe that the priest mentioned here may be Jean de Baeza, a Spanish Jesuit who arrived in Japan in 1590 and worked for thirty-six years in the Nagasaki area. See A. Halbout, "Souvenirs Chrétiens—'Les Séparés,'" *Bulletin de la Société des Missions-Etrangères de Paris* 5, no. 55 (juillet 1926): 410. Tagita says he was a Portuguese Jesuit. See SJSK, 169. All translations from French and Japanese are those of the author.

4 Halbout, 410–11. See also *Société des Missions-Etrangères de Paris, Compte Rendu des Travaux* (Paris: M.E.P., 1888), 25–26.

5 Halbout, 411.

6 Ryūsaku Tsunoda, William Theodore de Bary, and Donald Keene, comps., *Sources of Japanese Tradition*, vol. 1 (New York: Columbia University Press, 1964), 459–60.

7 Tagita, SJSK, 246–65.

8 Ibid., 265.

9 Ibid., 266–67. All biblical quotes used in this study are taken from *The New American Bible*, translated by members of the Catholic Biblical Association of America (New York, 1970).

10 Kōya Tagita, "Nihon no ichi noson ni okeru Kirisutokyō no bunka henyō" [Transformation of Christianity in a Japanese farming village], *Minzokugaku Kenkyū* [Journal of Ethnology] 18, no. 3 (1954): 196.

11 Kōya Tagita, "Some Aspects of Japanese-Christian Acculturation," in *Proceedings of the IXth International Congress on the History of Religions, Tokyo, 1958* (Tokyo, 1960), 446.

12 Tagita, SJSK, 274–75.

13 Ibid., 275.

[14] Masaharu Anesaki, *History of Japanese Religion* (Tokyo: Charles E. Tuttle Company, 1963), 46.

[15] Tagita, SJSK, 7–8.

[16] Kōya Tagita, "Study of Acculturation among the Secret Christians of Japan," private circulation by author (not dated), 126. I am grateful to Christal Whalen for pointing out to me that this move was initiated by the daimyō, not by the Christians fleeing for their lives.

[17] The job of the *chōkata* was to transpose each year the solar calendar of 1634 to the lunar calendar used by the Japanese.

[18] Tagita, SJSK, 61.

[19] Ibid.

[20] Ibid., 62.

[21] Furuno, *Kakure Kirishitan*, 102–3.

[22] Jennes, 14. There is a story that Koteda used to beat himself so mercilessly with a rope discipline that he had to be restrained. See Tagita, "Transformation of Christianity," 196.

[23] Furuno, *Kakure Kirishitan*, 103.

[24] Tagita, SJSK, 280.

[25] Furuno, *Kakure Kirishitan*, 124, 127–28.

[26] Ibid., 128.

[27] Ibid.

[28] Tagita, SJSK, 256–57.

[29] Furuno, *Kakure Kirishitan*, 130–31.

[30] Ibid., 132.

[31] Ibid., 125.

[32] Ichiro Hori, *Folk Religion in Japan: Continuity and Change*, ed. Joseph M. Kitagawa and Alan L. Miller (Chicago: University of Chicago Press, 1968), 38.

³³ Furuno, *Kakure Kirishitan*, 149–50; Tagita, "Acculturation among the Secret Christians," 128, 131, n.2.

³⁴ Furuno, *Kakure Kirishitan*, 132–33.

³⁵ Tagita, SJSK, 256.

³⁶ Furuno, *Kakure Kirishitan*, 125.

³⁷ Chie Nakane, *Japanese Society* (Berkeley: University of California Press, 1970), 29.

³⁸ Furuno, *Kakure Kirishitan*, 126–27.

³⁹ Ibid., 136. See also Kiyoto Furuno, "Kirishitan kazoku ni okeru no gireiteki shinzoku kankei" [Ritual kinship in Kirishitan families], *Minzokugaku Kenkyū* [Journal of Ethnology] 12 (April 21, 1957): 78–88.

⁴⁰ Furuno, *Kakure Kirishitan*, 139.

⁴¹ Carmen Blacker, *The Catalpa Bow: A Study of Shamanistic Practices in Japan* (London: George Allen & Unwin Ltd., 1975), 212.

⁴² Furuno, *Kakure Kirishitan*, 143–44.

⁴³ Ibid., 144.

⁴⁴ Hori, 16.

# Chapter 3

¹ Tagita, SJSK, 292–93.

² Ibid., 293. Kataoka Yakichi, using the same system, has the determination of the seventh-month feast occurring first. Therefore, if we use the same dates, in his calculation, the seventh month Jibiriya would occur on the eighteenth day, and the ninth month Otobarai, on the twenty-first day. See Kataoka, 193.

³ Tagita, SJSK, 297; Kataoka, 196.

⁴ Tagita, SJSK, 297–98.

⁵ Ibid., 298.

[6] Ibid.

[7] Furuno, *Kakure Kirishitan*, 161.

[8] Blacker, 48.

[9] Tagita, SJSK, 283–84.

[10] Ibid., 317–18.

[11] Furuno, *Kakure Kirishitan*, 153.

[12] Hori, 55.

[13] Furuno, *Kakure Kirishitan*, 155.

[14] Ibid., 155.

[15] Tagita, SJSK, 313–14.

[16] Kataoka, 194.

[17] Furuno, *Kakure Kirishitan*, 159.

[18] Tagita, SJSK, 284.

[19] Anesaki, 44.

[20] Furuno, *Kakure Kirishitan*, 156. Tagita places the Kazadome no gandate on the eighteenth day of the sixth month, and says that the principal Kaze no gandate was celebrated on the same day throughout Ikitsuki in the sixth month. See Tagita, SJSK, 314.

[21] Tagita, SJSK, 288. Furuno calls this festival Onagusama matsuri (amusement festival). See Furuno, *Kakure Kirishitan*, 159.

[22] Tagita, SJSK, 288–89. For details of the records kept for this festival in 1942 and 1950, see Tagita, "Nandogami omatsuri tōjisha no kiroku" [Records of secret Kirishitan festival by the participants], *Academia* 10 (June 1955), 175–92.

[23] Tagita, SJSK, 290–91.

[24] Furuno, *Kakure Kirishitan*, 156.

[25] Ibid., 154.

[26] Ibid.

27 Ibid., 157.

28 Tagita, SJSK, 312.

29 Hori, 21.

30 Tagita, SJSK, 406. A recording of some of the prayers of the Ikitsuki and Hirado Kirishitan is available commercially. It is titled "Kakure Kirishitan," Philips Records (Ph-7516–17), 1973. The recording was supervised by Kataoka Yakichi.

31 Laures, 64.

32 Tagita, SJSK, 380.

33 Kōya Tagita, "Kirisutokyō no Nihonteki bunka henyō" [Acculturation of Christianity in Japan], *Shukyō Kenkyū* [Journal of Religious Studies] 155 (March 1958): 443–44.

34 Ibid., 445.

35 Ibid., 448.

36 Blacker, 95.

37 Ibid., 97.

38 Tagita, SJSK, 345–46. For the music, see Kataoka, 146.

# Chapter 4

1 Francisque Marnas, *La Religion de Jésus ressuscitée au Japon dans la seconde moitié du XIX^e siècle*, vol. 1 (Paris: Delhomme et Briquet, 1896), 507.

2 Jennes, 204, n. 181.

3 Tagita, "Acculturation among the Secret Christians," 34.

4 The resume given here is based on the English translation of the text made by Tagita and distributed privately. It is found in "Acculturation among the Secret Christians," 38–84, along with the Japanese text. For the biblical version of the story, one might read the books of Genesis and Exodus and the gospel accounts of Matthew, Mark, and Luke in any standard Bible. The text is also available in *Kirishitan*

*sho, hai-yo sho* [Kirishitan and anti-Christian writings], ed. Ebisawa Arimichi et al., *Nihon shisō taikei* 25 (Tokyo: Iwanami, 1970), 381–409. There is a German translation by Alfred Bohner in *Monumenta Nipponica* 1.2:173–207 (July 1938).

5 Tagita observes that the Philippine Islands were made known to the Japanese by the missionaries and traders of the sixteenth and seventeenth centuries. "Acculturation among the Secret Christians,"49.

6 Tagita sees this as the river that was made famous in the battle of the Genji and Heike families. Ibid., 53. It may also come from the Latin *ave* and refer to Mary (Ave Maria).

7 Ibid., 56.

8 The text has Judatsu eating as usual on Wednesday morning before going to betray Jesus. Tagita thinks that this may refer to his breaking the Wednesday fast that is observed, along with Friday, among some of the kakure Kirishitan. Ibid., 68–69.

9 Ibid., 76.

10 Kōya Tagita, "Meeting of Religions in the *Tenchi Hajimari no Koto*," paper prepared for the XXVII International Congress of Orientalists (University of Michigan, 1967), 3. Given to me by Tagita, summer 1975.

11 Ibid., 3–4.

12 Ibid., 5.

13 Tagita, "Acculturation among the Secret Christians," 43.

14 Tagita, "Meeting of Religions," 4–5.

15 Tagita, "Acculturation among the Secret Christians," 53.

16 Ibid., 46.

17 Tsunoda, de Bary, and Keene, 29–30.

18 Ibid., 18.

19 Ibid.

# Chapter 5

1 Boxer, 401.

2 The status of the Ryūkyūs at this time was ambiguous. "Although China asserted suzerainty over the islands, they were in fact a dependency of the daimyō of Satsuma, who had conquered the islands in 1609. The semi-independent king paid tribute to Peking as well as to Satsuma." Jennes. See Jean Guennou, *Les Missions-Etrangères* (Paris: Editions St. Paul, 1963), 270; and Adrien Launey, *Histoire générale de la Société des Missions-Etrangères* (Paris: Téqui Libraire, 1894).

3 Marnas, I:320.

4 For the text of this proscription, see Jennes, 116–18.

5 See Marnas, I:342 ff.

6 *Annales de l'Association de la Société de la Propagation de la Foi*, vol. 37 (Lyons, 1865), 408.

7 Gordon A. Craig, *Europe Since 1815* (Hinsdale, Illinois: The Dryden Press, 1974), 106.

8 H. Daniel-Rops, *The Church in an Age of Revolution, 1789–1870*, trans. John Warrington (New York: E. P. Dutton & Co., Inc., 1965), 283–84.

9 Ibid., 284. The pope was declared infallible on July 18, 1870.

10 Marnas, I:488.

11 Ibid.

12 *Journal du Père Renaut*, in the library of the Seminary of St. Sulpice, Fukuoka, Japan.

13 *Les Missions Catholiques* XIII (Lyons, 1881), 113. There is a moving letter in the M.E.P. Archives from a young man, M. Leblanc, to Msgr. Petitjean (June 30, 1875), indicating that he is unable to learn the Japanese language. The task assigned by Petitjean to test language ability was to translate into colloquial Japanese the second chapter of the Book of Tobias from the Bible. Leblanc had twenty days to complete the task. He says, "I am humiliated to be so

incapable after having given up all to become a mission-ary." On July 27, 1875, Petitjean asked the M.E.P. superiors in Paris to take back Leblanc. I did not pursue the issue to see what became of the young man. M.E.P. Archives, Rue de Bac, Paris.

14 Marnas, I:550–51.

15 Ibid., 550–53. Their catechism was entitled *Seikyō yōri mondō* [A catechism of Christian doctrine in questions and answers].

16 Ibid., 553. The title of Petitjean's catechism was *Seikyō sho gaku yori* [A fundamental catechism of Christian doctrine].

17 Different dates are given for this event. Marnas gives October 21, 1866 (see vol. I, 571), and June 22 is given by Joseph L. van Hecken, C.I.C.M., in *The Catholic Church in Japan since 1859*, trans. John van Hoydonck, O.M.I. (Tokyo: Herder Agency, 1963), 22. From 1875 on, Petitjean wavered in his insistence on the use of Kirishitan terminology and allowed for a catechism in Chinese terminology.

18 The Daijokan order for the removal of the signboards reads as follows: "'From now on, in order that the people may have thorough knowledge of them, official proclamations shall be posted in a convenient place for thirty days. Continue to publicize proclamations in your jurisdiction as you have in the past. The signboards which have been posted until now, because their content is common knowl-edge, shall be taken down.'" In Thomas W. Burkman, "The Urakami Incident and the Struggle for Religious Toleration in Early Meiji Japan," *Japanese Journal of Religious Studies* I, no. 2, 3 (June–September 1974), 205.

19 Société des Missions-Etrangères de Paris, *Compte Rendu des Travaux* (Paris: M.E.P., 1879), 16. Hereafter cited as C.R.

20 C.R., 1882, 17–18.

21 Ibid., 1887, 47.

22 Abe Yoshiya, "Religious Freedom under the Meiji Consti-tution," *Contemporary Religion in Japan* IX, no. 4 (December 1968), 318. Thomas Burkman, op. cit., argues that diplo-

matic efforts were significant only as catalysts, and that Japan on its own was moving in the direction of religious toleration in early Meiji. There is interesting correspondence between the French Minister, Léon Roches, and Msgr. Petitjean in 1867 (August–October) regarding the persecutions the Christians were experiencing. Roches pleaded with the missionaries to curtail their zeal somewhat and obey the laws of Japan while Petitjean pleaded with Roches to intercede for the Christians. M.E.P. Archives, Paris.

[23] Laures, 134.

[24] Ibid., 133.

[25] Marnas, II:542. The first order of religious women to arrive in Japan was Soeurs de l'instruction charitable du Saint Enfant. Two other orders arrived in 1877 and 1878, also from France (Congrégation de l'Infant Jésus de Chauffailles and Congrégation des Soeurs de Saint Paul de Chartres).

[26] C.R., 1886, 5; 1878, 12; 1880, 17; 1882, 19; 1885, 38; 1887, 45, 47; 1888, 22; 1896, 63. See also *Les Missions Catholiques* XIII, 1881, 113; XXI, 1889, 386.

[27] C.R., 1886, 26; 1887, 39–41, 45–46; 1888, 28–29; 1892, 41–42; 1894, 66. See *Les Missions Catholiques* XXI, 182, 386.

[28] J. B. Chaillet, *Msgr. Petitjean 1829–1884 et la résurrection Catholique du Japon au XIX^e Siècle* (Montceau–Les–Mains, 1919), 149–50.

[29] Ibid., 151.

[30] Jennes, 204.

[31] C.R., 1878, 12.

[32] *Annales de l'Association de la Société de la Propagation de la Foi* 53 (Lyons, 1881), 249.

[33] C.R., 1886, 23.

[34] C.R., 1887, 39.

[35] C.R., 1888, 25.

[36] *Les Missions Catholiques* XIX, 1887, 101.

37 C.R., 1888, 27–28.

38 van Hecken, 32.

39 C.R., 1880, 19.

40 C.R., 1888, 22.

41 *Les Missions Catholiques* XXIII, 1891 606–10.

42 See Boxer and Elison.

43 Boxer, 375.

44 Ibid., 377.

45 Elison, 217–18.

46 C.R., 1893, 62.

47 C.R., 1893, 58

48 C.R., 1894, 74.

49 *Les Missions Catholiques* XXXII, 1900, 482. Article 28 of the Meiji Constitution granted religious freedom to Japanese subjects so long as it did not upset the peace and order of the realm or conflict with their duties as subjects. "Religious toleration in a more unrestricted sense did not achieve legal standing until the 1946 constitution and the 1951 Religious Juridical Persons Law (Shūkyō hōjin hō)"; see Burkman, 146.

50 C.R., 1905, 14.

51 C.R., 1906, 17–18.

52 C.R., 1911, 20.

53 See Irwin Scheiner, *Christian Converts and Social Protest in Meiji Japan*, (Berkeley: University of California Press, 1970), and John F. Howes, "Japanese Christians and American Missionaries," in *Changing Japanese Attitudes toward Modernization*, ed. Marius B. Jansen (Princeton: Princeton University Press, 1965), 337–68.

# Chapter 6

[1] Based on figures given in Marnas, II:543.

[2] Cited in Madson, 1.

[3] Ibid.

[4] Blacker, 33.

[5] Earhart, 5.

[6] Ibid., 5–6.

[7] Ibid., 6.

[8] Ibid., 6–7.

[9] Ibid., 7.

[10] Ibid., 8.

# Chapter 7

[1] One lead suggested, which I have not followed up yet, is to compare the kakure Kirishitan to the Fujufuse Nichiren Buddhist believers who were forced into seclusion at the end of the sixteenth century. It would be interesting to compare the metamorphosis of Christianity with the kakure Kirishitan to the development of Buddhism with the Fujufuse Nichiren sect.

[2] See Irwin Scheiner for a discussion of Christian samurai.

[3] "Christianity in the Japanese Rural Community: Acceptance and Rejection" in his *Religion in Changing Japanese Society* (Tokyo: Tokyo University Press, 1970), 117–33.

[4] Ibid., 119. Two points of interest: (1) Annaka is the home village of Niijima Jō (1843–91), the founder of Dōshisha University; (2) According to Irokawa Daikichi, the Methodist Episcopal church was known "even among Protestant sects, for its fervent social activism. Many of its members went on to join the People's Rights, peace, and social reform movements." See Daikichi Irokawa, *The*

*Culture of the Meiji Period*, trans. Marius B. Jansen (Princeton: Princeton University Press, 1985), 92.

5 Ibid., 121.

6 Ibid., 122.

7 Ibid., 125.

8 Ibid., 126, 127.

9 Ibid., 133. Other reasons why there were not more converts to Christianity are the growing influence of the emperor system and Japanese nationalism; the nonaccommodating orthodoxy of Christianity as compared with Japan's syncretic approach to religion; the emphasis on rational, scientific thought that came with modernization; and the awareness that Western success and power were available without Christianity.

10 Ibid., 121.

11 *Christianity the Japanese Way* (Leiden: E. J. Brill, 1979). Uchimura was converted to Christianity at the Sapporo Agricultural School, which was under the direction of William Clarke. He converted as a result of peer pressure from his classmates, but eventually Christianity became the overriding concern in his life.

12 Ibid., 6–7.

13 Ibid., 7.

14 Ibid., 8.

15 Tatsuo Arima, *The Failure of Freedom: A Portrait of Modern Japanese Intellectuals* (Cambridge: Harvard University Press, 1969), 33–34.

16 Ibid., 190.

17 Ibid., 21, 24. Robert Bellah explains his Bushidō (the way of the warrior) as idealized Kantian Bushidō "in which the element of selfless duty has been extricated from the particular nexus of feudal relationships." "Ienaga Saburō and the Search for Meaning in Modern Japan," in Jansen, 412. See also, Caldarola, 57.

18 Caldarola, 209.

19 Ibid, 193. The full name of the movement is Genshin Fukuin Undō (Original Gospel Movement).

20 "Japanese Christianity: Between Orthodoxy and Heterodoxy," in *Authority and the Individual in Japan* (Tokyo: Tokyo University Press, 1978), 98. Uchimura would totally reject that classification because he did not believe in "sects" and what "he wanted most of all was to be independent of any denomination or sect." See Takeo Doi, "Uchimura Kanzō: Japanese Christianity in Comparative Perspective," in *Japan, A Comparative View*, ed. Albert Craig (Princeton: Princeton University Press, 1979), 182.

21 Ibid., 89.

22 Ibid., 91.

23 Ibid.

24 Ibid., 98.

25 Ibid.

26 Ibid., 106.

27 Ibid. He was at one time a member of the Mukyōkai.

28 Ibid., 107.

29 Ibid., 103, 106.

30 Ibid., 101.

# Conclusion

1 One exception to this statement was the conversion to Ōmotokyō (an offshoot of Shintō) of 150 kakure of Fukuejima, in the Gotō Islands in 1961. See "Shintō Wins over Maria Kannon," The *Yomiuri* (Japan), November 6, 1961, 8.

2 Yosei Amano, "'Kakure Kirishitan,' Descendants of Persecuted Christians Still Faithful," *The Mainichi Daily News* (Japan), December 31, 1968.

3 Shinmichi Yasomatsu, interviewed in Higashikaskiyama, Sotome, Japan, August 9, 1975.

4 Based on interviews with Tagita Kōya, Nagoya, July 18, 1975; Furuno Kiyoto, Tokyo, August 5, 1975; and Kataoka Yakichi, Nagasaki, August 8–9, 1975.

5 Walter M. Abbott, S.J., ed., *The Documents of Vatican II* (New York: Guild Press, 1966), 610–11.

## Epilogue

1 From *The Gates of the Forest* by Elie Wiesel. Copyright ©1964 by Editions du Seuil. English translation Copyright ©1966 by Holt, Rinehart and Winston. Reprinted by permission of Henry Holt and Co., Inc.

# Glossary

## Japanese Terms Used More than Once

| | | |
|---|---|---|
| bakufu | 幕府 | Military government under the control of a shōgun. |
| bateren | 伴天連 | Name given to the Catholic missionaries by the Japanese. From the Portuguese *padre*. |
| butsudan | 仏壇 | The Buddhist household altar. |
| chōkata | 帳方 | The calendar maker of the Kirishitan in Kurosaki and the Gotō Islands. |
| compania | コンパンヤ | Religious groupings on the islands of Ikitsuki and Hirado, dating back to the religious organizations begun by the missionaries in the sixteenth and seventeenth centuries. From the Portuguese *companhia*. |
| daimyō | 大名 | Literally, "great name." Title given to local lords who ruled over semiautonomous domains (*han*) during the Tokugawa period (1603–1868). |
| dōjuku | 同宿 | "Fellow lodger"; term used by the sixteenth- and seventeenth-century missionaries for Japanese who were asked to preach and catechize. The dōjuku were not religious but dedicated their services to the church. |

| | | |
|---|---|---|
| erenja | エレンジャ | Heresy, from the Portuguese *heresia*. The kakure Kirishitan called those who were not kakure Kirishitan *erenjamon*. |
| fure | 触 | Geographical areas; subdivisions of a village. |
| gobanyaku | 御番役 | The highest official in charge of a tsumoto in Ikitsuki. |
| goningumi | 五人組 | Groupings consisting of five families responsible for mutual surveillance; begun during the Tokugawa period. |
| gozensama | ごぜん様 | One of the categories of nandogami consisting of hanging scrolls or banners that depict Christ, Mary, or one of the saints or martyrs. |
| higurichō | 日繰帳 | The calendar of the kakure Kirishitan in Kurosaki and the Gotō Islands. |
| kambō | 看防 | Professional lay helpers or church guardians who often acted in the place of the priests, leading prayers, calling the priests for those who were ill, and performing baptisms. |
| kamidana | 神棚 | The Shintō household altar. |
| kō | 講 | Fraternity or religious association. |
| mideshi | み弟子 | Disciple, head of the compania in Ikitsuki and Hirado. |
| mizukata | 水方 | Baptizer for the Kirishitan of Kurosaki and the Gotō Islands. |

| | | |
|---|---|---|
| nandogami | 納戸神 | Literally "closet gods," religious articles treasured by the Kirishitan of Ikitsuki and Hirado. |
| nibanyaku | 二番役 | The second-ranking official in charge of a tsumoto in Ikitsuki and Hirado. |
| ofuda | お礼 | Charms or small pieces of wood used by the Kirishitan in Ikitsuki and Hirado. The wooden pieces represent the fifteen mysteries of the rosary and the "amen." |
| omaburi | おまぶり | Small pieces of paper cut in the form of a cross and used as charms to protect fields, homes, and persons. |
| oshikae | おしかえ | The ceremony of drawing out an ofuda. |
| otempensia | おテンペンシャ | Originally, an object used to inflict physical pain on one-self as a means of religious discipline, evolving eventually to a bundle a hemp rope used to bless and cure. From the Portuguese *penitença,* penance. |
| samurai | 侍 | Warrior. |
| sanbanyaku | 三番役 | The third-ranking official in charge of a tsumoto in Ikitsuki and Hirado. |
| San Juan-sama | サンジュワン | The name given to the holy water found on Nakae no shima, used for baptisms. |
| sazukeyaku | 授け役 | Baptizer for the Kirishitan of Ikitsuki and Hirado. |

| | | |
|---|---|---|
| shōgun | 将軍 | Military leader who headed the bakufu. |
| tamoto kami | たもと神 | Sleeve gods of the kakure Kirishitan on Ikitsuki and Hirado. Referred to religious objects that could be tucked unobserved into the kimono sleeve, such as a rosary. |
| tsumoto | つもと | The home that contained the nandogami in Ikitsuki and Hirado. |

# Kirishitan Place Names Mentioned in the Text

| | |
|---|---|
| 馬場 | Baba |
| 御崎 | Gosaki |
| 五島 | Gotō Islands |
| 平戸 | Hirado |
| 本触 | Honshoku |
| 一部浦 | Ichibu-ura |
| 生月 | Ikitsuki |
| 黒崎 | Kurosaki |
| 森岳崎 | Moridakesaki |
| 中江島 | Nakae no shima |
| 境目 | Sakaime |
| 里 | Sato |
| 正田 | Shoda |
| 外海 | Sotome |
| 館浦 | Tachiura |
| 山田 | Yamada |

# Bibliography

Abbott, Walter M., S.J., ed. *The Documents of Vatican II.* New York: Guild Press, 1966.

Amano, Yosei. "'Kakure Kirishitan,' Descendants of Persecuted Christians Still Faithful." *The Mainichi Daily News,* December 30–31, 1968.

Anesaki, Masaharu. *A Concordance to the History of Kirishitan Missions.* Proceedings of the Imperial Academy, supplement to vol. VI. Tokyo: Office of the Academy, 1930.

——. *History of Japanese Religion.* Tokyo: Charles E. Tuttle Company, 1963.

*Annales de l'Association de la Propagation de la Foi.* Lyons.

*Annales de la Société des Missions-Etrangères et de l'oeuvre des Partants.* Paris.

Archives, Société des Missions-Etrangères de Paris, Rue de Bac, Paris.

Arima, Tatsuo. *The Failure of Freedom: A Portrait of Modern Japanese Intellectuals.* Cambridge: Harvard University Press, 1969.

Blacker, Carmen. *The Catalpa Bow: A Study of Shamanistic Practices in Japan.* London: George Allen & Unwin Ltd., 1975.

Boxer, Charles Ralph. *The Christian Century in Japan, 1549–1650.* Berkeley: University of California Press, 1951.

Boyle, Donald, S.F.M. "The Strange Story of the Hanare." *Scarboro Missions* (July–August 1975): 8–11.

Bray, William D. "The Hidden Christians of Ikitsuki Island." *The Japan Christian Quarterly* 26 (April 1960): 76–84.

Brou, Alexandre. *Saint François Xavier: Conditions et methodes de son apostolat.* Paris: A. Giraudon, 1925.

Burkman, Thomas W. "The Urakami Incident and the Struggle for Religious Toleration in Early Meiji Japan." *Japanese*

*Journal of Religious Studies* I, no. 2, 3 (June–September 1974): 143–216.

Caldarola, Carlo. *Christianity the Japanese Way.* Leiden: E. J. Brill, 1979.

Chaillet, J. B. Msgr. *Petitjean 1829–1884 et la résurrection Catholique du Japon au XIX^e siècle.* Montceau-les-Mains, 1919.

Cieslik, Hubert, S.J. "Early Jesuit Missionaries in Japan (II): Balthasar Gago and Japanese Christian Terminology." *Missionary Bulletin* 8 (May–June 1954): 82–90.

*Compte Rendu des Travaux de la Société des Missions-Etrangères.* Paris.

Cooper, Michael, S.J., ed. *The Southern Barbarians: The First Europeans in Japan.* Tokyo: Kodansha International Ltd., 1971.

Craig, Gordon A. *Europe Since 1815.* Hinsdale, Illinois: The Dryden Press, 1974.

Daniel-Rops, Henri. *The Church in an Age of Revolution, 1789–1870.* Trans. John Warrington. New York: E. P. Dutton & Co., Inc., 1965.

Doi, Takeo. "Uchimura Kanzō: Japanese Christianity in Comparative Perspective." In *Japan: A Comparative View*, ed. Albert Craig. Princeton: Princeton University Press, 1979.

Earhart, H. Byron. *Japanese Religion: Unity and Diversity.* The Religious Life of Man Series. Belmont, California: Dickenson Publishing Company, Inc., 1969.

Eberhardt, Newman C., C.M. *A Summary of Catholic History.* Vol. 2 St. Louis: B. Herder Book Co., 1962.

Ebisawa, Arimichi. "Crypto-Christianity in Tokugawa Japan." *Japan Quarterly* 7, no. 3 (July–September 1960): 288–94.

Ebisawa, Arimichi, H. Cieslik, Doi Tadai, and Ōtsuka Mitsunobu, eds. *Kirishitan sho, hai-yo sho* キリシタン書非耶書 [Kirishitan and anti-Christian writings]. *Nihon shisō taikei* 日本思想大系 25. Tokyo: Iwanami, 1970.

Elison, George. *Deus Destroyed, The Image of Christianity in Early Modern Japan.* Cambridge: Harvard University Press, 1973.

Furuno, Kiyoto. 古野清人. "Kirishitan kazoku ni okeru gireiteki shinzoku kankei—Padrinazgo-no hikaku kenkyū キリシタン家族における儀礼的親族関係 — Padrinazgoの 比較研究 [Comparative study of ritual kinship in Kirishitan families with Padrinazgo]. *Minzokugaku Kenkyū*民族学研究 [Journal of Ethnology] 12 (April 21, 1957): 79–88.

——.*Kakure Kirishitan* 隠れ キリシタン [Hidden Christians]. Tokyo: Shibundo, 1959.

——.Interview with author. Subject's home, Tokyo, Japan, August 5, 1975.

Guennou, Jean. *Les Missions-Etrangères.* Paris: Editions St. Paul, 1963.

Halbout, A. "Souvenirs Chrétiens—'Les Séparés.'" *Bulletin de la Société des Missions-Etrangères de Paris* 5, no. 55. (juillet 1926): 397–411.

Hartman, Arnuf, O.S.A. *The Augustinians in Seventeenth Century Japan.* King City: Ontario, 1965.

Hori, Ichiro. *Folk Religion in Japan: Continuity and Change.* Ed. Joseph M. Kitagawa and Alan L. Miller. Chicago: University of Chicago Press, 1968.

Hughes, Philip. *A Popular History of the Catholic Church.* New York: Macmillan Company, 1949.

Humbertclaude, P. "La litterature chrétienne au Japon il y a trois cents ans." *Bulletin de la Maison Franco-Japonaise* 8, no. 2–4 (Tokyo, 1937): 158–220.

Irokawa, Daikichi. *The Culture of the Meiji Period.* Trans. Marius B. Jansen. Princeton: Princeton University Press, 1985.

Jansen, Marius B., ed. *Changing Japanese Attitudes toward Modernization.* Princeton: Princeton University Press, 1965.

Jennes, Joseph, C.I.C.M. *A History of the Catholic Church in Japan from its Beginnings to the Early Meiji Era, 1549–1873.* Revised ed. Tokyo: Oriens Institute for Religious Research, 1973.

*Journal du Père Renaut.* Seminary of St. Sulpice, Fukuoka, Japan.

"Kakure Kirishitan Make the Headlines." *Tosei News,* November 24, 1961.

Kataoka, Yakichi. 片岡弥吉 *Kakure Kirishitan rekishi to minzoku* かくれキリシタン歴史と民俗 [Hidden Christians: history and customs]. Tokyo: Nihon Hōsō Shuppan Kyōkai, 1967.

——. Interview with author. Catholic Center, Nagasaki, Japan, August 8–9, 1975.

Kitagawa, Joseph M. *Religion in Japanese History.* New York: Columbia University Press, 1966.

"Konchirisan no ryaku" こんちりさんのりやく [Compendium of Contrition]. Photocopy.

Launey, Adrien. *Histoire générale de la Société des Missions-Etrangères.* 3 vols. Paris: Téqui Libraire, 1894.

Laures, Johannes, S.J., comp. *Kirishitan Bunko: A Manual of Books and Documents on the Early Christian Mission in Japan.* Monumenta Nipponica Monographs, no. 5., 3rd edition. Tokyo: Sophia University Press, 1957.

Lopez-Gay, Jesús, S.J. "The Pre-Evangelization in the First Years of the Japan Mission." *Missionary Bulletin* 18 (1964): 587–92.

——. *El catecumenado en la mision del Japon del XVI.* Rome: Pontifical Gregorian University, 1966.

Lu, David John. *Sources of Japanese History.* Vol. 1. New York: McGraw-Hill Book Company, 1974.

Madson, William. *Christo-Paganism: A Study of Mexican Religious Syncretism.* Reprinted from Publication 19, 105–80, Middle American Research Institute. New Orleans: Tulane University, 1957.

Marnas, Francisque, MEP. *La Religion de Jésus réssuscitée au Japon dans la seconde moitié du XIX$^e$ siècle.* 2 vols. Paris et Lyon: Delhomme et Briquet, 1896–97.

*Les Missions Catholiques.* Lyons: Bureau des Missions Catholiques.

Morioka, Kiyomori. "Christianity in the Japanese Rural Community: Acceptance and Rejection." In *Religion in Changing Japanese Society,* ed. Kiyomori Morioka, 117–33. Tokyo: Tokyo University Press, 1970.

Mourret, Fernand, S.S. *A History of the Catholic Church.* Vol. 5. Trans. Newton Thompson. St. Louis: B. Herder Book Co., 1930.

Murakami, Naojiro. "An Old Church Calendar in Japanese." *Monumenta Nipponica* 5, no. 1 (1942): 219–24.

Nakane, Chie. *Japanese Society.* Berkeley: University of California Press, 1970.

Pagés, Léon. *L'Histoire de la religion chrétienne au Japon depuis 1598 jusqu'à 1651.* 2 vols. Paris: Charles Dounial Libraire, 1869.

Sansom, George B. *The Western World and Japan.* New York: Alfred A. Knopf, 1950.

Scheiner, Irwin. *Christian Converts and Social Protest in Meiji Japan.* Berkeley: University of California Press, 1970.

Schütte, Josef Franz, S.J. *Valignano's Mission Principles for Japan.* 2 vols. Trans. John J. Coyne, S.J. St. Louis: The Institute of Sources, 1980.

Shibutani, Rev. J. "The Schismatics of Nagasaki." *Missionary Bulletin* 3, no. 1 (Spring 1949): 54–58.

"Shinto Wins over Maria Kannon." *Yomiuri,* November 6, 1961.

Steichen, M. *The Christian Daimyōs: A Century of Religious and Political History in Japan.* Trans. Francis McCullagh. Tokyo: R. Gakuin, n.d.

Tagita, Kōya. 田北耕也. "Nihon no ichi noson ni okeru Kirisutokyō no bunka henyō"日本の一農村におけるキリスト教の文化変容[Transformation of Christianity in a Japanese farming village]. *Minzokugaku Kenkyū* 民俗学研究 [Journal of Ethnology] 18, no. 3 (1954): 195–226.

——.*Shōwa jidai no sempuku Kirishitan* 昭和時代の潜伏キリシタン [Hidden Christians in the Showa era]. Tokyo: Nihon Gakujutsu Shinkokai, 1954.

———. "Nandogami omatsuri tōjisha no kiroku" 納戸神大祭 当事者 の記録 [Records of secret Kirishitan festival by the participants]. *Academia* アカデミヤ 10 (1955): 175–92.

———. "Secret Christians in Japan." *Missionary Bulletin* 10, no. 3 (1956): 253–57.

———. "Kirisutokyō no Nihonteki bunka henyō" キリスト教の日本的 文化 変容 [Acculturation of Christianity in Japan]. *Shukyō Kenkyū* [Journal of Religious Studies] 155 (March 1958): 438–61.

———. "Some Aspects of Japanese-Christian Acculturation." In *Proceedings of the IXth International Congress of the History of Religions, Tokyo, 1958,* 444–48. Tokyo: Maruzen, 1960.

———. "Meeting of Religions in the *Tenchi Hajimari no Koto.*" Paper prepared by the author for the XXVII International Congress of Orientalists, University of Michigan, 1967.

———. Interview with author. Nanzan University, Nagoya, Japan, July 18, 1975.

———. "Study of Acculturation among Secret Christians of Japan." Private distribution by the author, n.d.

Takeda, Kiyoko. "Japanese Christianity: Between Orthodoxy and Heterodoxy." In *Authority and the Individual in Japan.* Tokyo: Tokyo University Press, 1978.

Tsunoda, Ryūsaku, Wm. Theodore de Bary, and Donald Keene, comps. *Sources of Japanese Tradition.* Vol. I. New York: Columbia University Press, 1964.

Uyttenbroeck, Thomas, O.F.M. *Early Franciscans in Japan.* Missionary Bulletin Series, vol. 6. Himeji, Japan: Committee of the Apostolate, 1958.

van Hecken, Joseph L., C.I.C.M. *The Catholic Church in Japan since 1859.* Trans. and rev. John van Hoydonck, O.M.I. Tokyo: Herder Agency, 1963.

Verwilghen, A. F. "The 'Ave' of the Hidden Christians." *The Japan Missionary Bulletin* 15, no. 4 (May 1961): 238–41.

Yasomatsu, Shimichi. Interview with author. Subject's home, Higashikashi-yama, Sotome, Japan, August 9, 1975.

Yoshiya, Abe. "Religious Freedom under the Meiji Constitution."
*Contemporary Religions in Japan* IX, no. 4 (December 1968):
263–338.

# Index

Accommodation of non-Christian observances, 89, 102–3, 137, 146, 148
Acculturation, 151
Adultery, 111
Agiri (Easter) festival, 58, 61
Amagai festival, 67
Ancestors, importance to kakure Kirishitan of, *xiv,* 136
Anesaki, Masaharu, *xiii,* 39
Annaka Church (Congregational), 143–44, 146–47
Anointing the sick
  priest required for, 20, 22
  recitation of name of, 71
  substituting for priests in administering, 23
Apostasy of Japanese Christians, 28, 156–57
Arishima, Takeo, 156
Ashikaga shōgun, deposing of, 4
Augustinians, 118
  arrival in 1602 of, 171n.39

Baptism
  adaptations in administering, 16–17
  importance to kakure Kirishitan groups of, 50, 117, 133
  by lay people, 16, 20, 22, 129, 163
  missionaries' approach to converts, 9–10, 12, 114–15, 131
  by mizukata, 41–42
  recitation of name of, 71
  by sazukeyaku, 43, 49, 61
  taboos connected with, 49, 61
  water for, obtaining, 49
Basutean (Sebastian), 36–37, 117

Bateren (Catholic priests), 9
  ratio of converts to, 20, 170n.8
  return of, 99–103, 107
  rewards for turning in, 26
Bellah, Robert, 184n.17
Blacker, Carmen, 50, 71–72, 134
Boxer, C. R., 28, 119
Buddha, marks or ranks of, 87
Buddhism
  distinctiveness of Japanese, 134
  influence in nineteenth-century practices of the kakure Kirishitan, 120, 148
  influence in the *Tenchi hajimari no koto* of, 78, 87–89
  melding of other religions with, 134, 152–53
  membership requirement for families during Tokugawa period in, 27, 88
Buppō (Law of Hotoke), 8
Burial ceremonies, 146
Burkman, Thomas W., 180
Bushidō, 152, 184n.17
Butsudan (Buddhist household altar), 130, 135, 146, 159

Cabral, Francisco, 171n.25
  negative view of adaptation of, 15
  view on missionaries learning Japanese of, 16
Caldarola, Carlo, 151–53
Catholic church
  isolationism in nineteenth century of, 101–2, 109, 143
  self-scrutiny of, 3
Cerqueira, Luis
  length of stay of, 171n.32
  rules for administering baptism by, 17